HOW TO TURN YOUR ABILITY INTO CASH

HOW TO TURN YOUR ABILITY INTO CASH

Revised and Enlarged Edition

by

EARL PREVETTE, A.B., LL.B.

PRENTICE-HALL, INC.

Englewood Cliffs, N. J.

L.C. Cat. Card No.: 53-5698

First printing .... January, 1953
Second printing .... June, 1953
Third printing .... March, 1954
Fourth printing .... August, 1956
Fifth printing .... June, 1957
Sixth printing .... January, 1958
Seventh printing .... April, 1958

PRINTED IN THE UNITED STATES OF AMERICA

43562

This book is written for you.
It is dedicated to your ability.

CONTENTS

vii

CONTENTS

HOW TO TURN YOUR ABILITY INTO CASH

Chapter 1

IT MIGHT HAVE BEEN YOU

One day not long ago, while I was standing on the corner of a busy street in Philadelphia, talking to a friend, along came an old man. He was a decrepit old man with swollen, tearful eyes, and his unshaven face was drawn and withered. His lips were blue with unclean sores. His toes were pushing through his worn-out shoes. His clothes were torn to rags. He had seen better days. I thought, "How dreadfully poverty has gnawed at you." I was stunned for the moment. With a look of sadness, and with a dirty, bloated hand thrust forward, he pleaded for a few pennies. He got a few more pennies; I got a little more sense.

As I pondered over the circumstances that had caused the deplorable condition of this man, and had left him a wreck in its ruins, I began to think: "It might have been you!"

What happened to this old man? What started him toward his deplorable condition? What caused such poverty? Why had fortune turned into misfortune? His plight may have been due to overindulgence, to grief, to envy, to jealousy, to hatred, to prejudice, to dread, to self-pity, to temptation, or to discouragement Whatever it was, it had changed his outlook, his attitude, his process of thinking, and his entire pattern of living. Desperation, despair, discouragement, disappointment, sorrow, and sadness were indelibly stamped in the lines of his face. He was a picture of his thoughts, a victim of circumstances, and a slave to poverty.

Your Greatest Enemy

In analyzing the plight of this old man, I came to the conclusion that his condition was a definite result of that desperate little enemy—negative thinking.

Negative thinking is a sneaky little enemy that silently steals its way into a man's consciousness and, like a thief at night, steals not his purse but, through robbing him of power, makes him poor indeed. Negative thinking is a sinister influence that works night and day to prey on a man's soul. It is man's worst enemy, and life's meanest foe. It is worse than war, and largely the cause of war. It is the curse of the human race. It is as blind to reason as an owl is to light. It turns friends into enemies and enemies into foes. It robs a man of reason. It stirs up hate, greed, selfishness, cynicism, pessimism, anger, suspicion, rivalry, jealousy, revenge, lust, and envy. It tears down confidence, undermines health, impairs character, and causes poverty.

An old legend relates that the devil was thrown into bankruptcy. Out of all his tools, the creditors permitted him to keep one. The tool he selected was the wedge of negative thinking. Asked why he liked this tool better than all the rest, the devil explained, "It is because this is the one tool which I can use when all others fail. Let me get that little wedge into a man's consciousness, and it opens everything else. That wedge has opened more doors for me than all other weapons combined."

Someone asked one of the world's greatest explorers what exploration he enjoyed most. His answer was, "My personal preference is for sitting in an old-fashioned rocking chair and exploring the undiscovered regions inside my own mind."

In exploring the undiscovered regions inside the mind, man

discovers he has interest. His interest creates a desire. There are two kinds of desire. One is physical. One is mental. Subsistence and propagation satisfy the physical desire. Thoughts and ideas satisfy the mental desire.

How to Conquer Negative Thinking

There are two kinds of thoughts: positive thoughts, which are creative, and negative thoughts, which are destructive. I often compare positive thoughts to light, and negative thoughts to darkness. Darkness is nothing. It is the absence of light. Turn on the light, and there is no darkness.

Negative thoughts of dread, worry, anger, prejudice, jealousy, envy, grudge, stubbornness, impudence, selfishness, cynicism, gloom, hate, despair, and discouragement disappear instantly when they meet the positive thoughts of love, faith, consideration, respect, kindness, courage, understanding, persistence, fervor, loyalty, joy, power, plenty, endurance, and strength. Think positive thoughts, and the ability can accomplish any desire.

Positive thoughts are based on understanding and faith. Negative thoughts are based on ignorance and doubt. There is no problem or condition that fails to disappear in the light of positive thoughts. Face one half of your problems or troubles with positive thoughts, and they will disappear, and then face the other half, and they will disappear. Positive and creative thinking will burn holes in problems, as a lighted cigarette will burn holes in tissue paper.

In the study of physics we find Ohm's Law of Electricity. It teaches: $C = \frac{E}{R}$. C is the current or the amount of electrical energy to be delivered for any given purpose. E is the power-house to supply the current. R is the resistance the current meets on its way to do the job. The less resistance offered to the current, the more electrical energy available to do the job. This depends on the efficiency of the conductor.

The same applies to you. You are a conductor for your thoughts. Ability is the powerhouse. Positive thoughts are the current. Negative thoughts are the resistance. Get rid of all negative thoughts. Get rid of resistance. Get rid of all inhibitions, all grudges, and all dreads. Your ability demonstrates its full power and strength when unhampered, and unencumbered by resistance. Your income, your health, your well-being, your happiness, and your peace of mind are only retarded by permitting the phantoms of negative thinking to set up a resistance to your ability.

A physician in Boston examined twenty-five people suffering from inflammatory disorders. A close check-up revealed that every one of them was holding a grudge. Negative thinking impairs the body and also disrupts the ability.

Cut loose and free yourself from all petty restrictions, all pygmy notions, and all corroded resistance. They retard and hold you back. Open up the channel to good. Cast out all your troubles. What good are they? Turn the power and dominion of positive thoughts on worries and dreads, and they are gone. Seek good and expect nothing but good. Rejoice and be glad. It liberates and frees you. You cease to dread; you cease to worry. You feel like a new person. You feel like starting all over again. What seemed a burden and a task is turned into a pleasant and interesting adventure

Conditions are thought-made; change your thoughts and you change your conditions. Therefore, if your conditions seem unbearable, dark, and gloomy, change your thoughts about them and see how quickly your thoughts change you.

J. Allen Boone in his book, *Letters to Strongheart*, reveals the qualities and attributes of a German Shepherd dog who became a movie star. The book sums up the character of this wonderful dog as follows: He put everything he had in everything he did. All his acts were positive and decided. He spared nothing. He gave all. This teaches a great lesson. Whatever you do, put your all into it. Lose yourself in what you are seeking to accomplish. Give all and there is no room for negative thoughts.

How to Succeed Through Positive Thinking

Therefore, the remedy for negative thinking is positive thoughts. The application of positive thoughts floods the consciousness with faith, confidence, dominion, and determination and gives you the power to perform with decision, precision, skill, and speed. Think positive, be positive, and act positive, and negative thinking goes out the window. One mighty breath from Truth will scatter negative thinking and all its hosts of human mockeries and miseries like a whirlwind and establish the reign of positive thoughts that assure success in any endeavor.

How to Create Ability

Positive thoughts will knock out your worst enemy—negative thinking. The preparation is now laid for your best friend—Ability. Ability is positive thoughts on the job to deliver to you the things you desire.

There is a tide in the affairs of men which when taken at the flood leads on to fortune. That tide is the accumulation of positive thoughts that must eventually burst forth into a flood of good fortune.

Emerson said, "We lie in the lap of immense intelligence which makes us receivers of its truth, and organs of its activity." All around and about us this vital force and creative power is instantly available for us to draw from, and to apply to our activities to supply all our human needs. It is God's gift to man. It is not owned by any one man, or any group of men. It is the property of all men. However, to be of practical value, each individual must seek it, recognize it, realize it, and demonstrate it for himself in his own affairs. It is positive and active and can develop all the faculties and talents of the individual into ability capable of achievement.

"*Cogito, ergo sum.* I think, therefore I am." The power to think gives man the ability to analyze his own thought. Thought is not an indefinite abstraction, but a vital, living force, the most vital, subtle and irresistible force in the world. Thought has form, quality and substance. Thought can originate, develop and create things.

In developing the ability to think and create things to satisfy man's desire, it is wise to get the right attitude. Man is greater than the flesh and bones that carry him around. His body belongs to him, but he does not belong to his body. The power to think does not confine him to his own skin. He can project thought. He can visualize and create things to satisfy his mental desires. To do this scientifically and effectively it is essential to organize his thoughts into a plan. This book is an example.

How to Turn Your Desires into Action

What is a plan? A plan is a method of action, procedure or arrangement. It is a program to be done. It is a design to give effect to an idea, a thought, a project or the development of something.

A plan may ask: What do you desire? Do you desire to sell something? Do you desire a job? Do you desire an increase in salary? Do you desire clients? Do you desire customers? Do you desire to invent something? These questions pertain to your present or future occupation. The only way to make your desire known is through a plan. It conveys to people in plain language a definite concept of what you are offering for their consideration.

My book, *How to Sell by Telephone*, tells how I sold $10,-000,000 worth of life insurance to strangers over the telephone. To achieve this unparalleled record, it was necessary for me to create a plan to satisfy my desire. The plan set forth in plain, understandable language the value and advantages of life insurance, and what they meant to the prospect. After creating the plan it was necessary to develop a process to put the plan into action. This required faith to believe wholeheartedly in the plan, repetition to perfect it, imagination to visualize it, and persistence to see it through. Finally, it required the act to idealize the plan, to feel its possession and claim it as reality. I put all the power at my command in the plan and the desire was satisfied.

Self-discipline, self-knowledge, self-improvement, self-expression and self-unfoldment are individual undertakings. The word "individual" comes from two Latin words—"in," which means "not," and "divisus," which means "divisible." An individual is not divisible. He is a complete entity, a self-contained unit, made up of four parts. One part is matter—the physical body to house him. One part is essence to give him form and to identify him according to his species. One part is mind to guide and direct him. One part is spirit to inspire and to enthuse him. Strict attention and careful consideration must be given each part. The physical body must have the proper food. The essence must be treated with care. The mind must be fed with positive thoughts. The spirit must be inspired with unfaltering faith. When these four parts are well fed and well

treated, harmony prevails; and the individual functions health-
fully, generates happiness and produces wealth.

How to turn your ability into Cash puts the Law of Wealth
into operation. When applied it never fails to produce an
abundance of worldly goods.

In applying the ideas and suggestions in this book it will
enhance your ability to realize three things.

Ideas and Suggestions You Can Use

First: Realize that everything you can think of exists now;
otherwise you could not think about it. There is no lack of anything and there should be no envy or jealousy between men.
There is enough of everything for everyone that lives.

Second: Realize that all things belong to God's creation and
that you can only have temporary use of them. There is no
limit on your desires, and you can have the use of anything
the ability can create.

Third: Realize that all things are distributed to those who
have desires, but ability must be applied to formulate plans to
claim these desires.

Here are a few suggestions that will help you stake your
claim.

Things to Do

1. Meditate and ask God if there is any reason why you
should not have the thing you desire. Dismiss your desire for a
few days and if it is right for you to have it, the desire will
become more intense. This removes doubt and uncertainty, and
inspires determination and action.

2. Make a strong mental picture of what you desire, and
affirm it several times each day.

3. Be specific about what you desire.

If you desire money, visualize the amount and feel it in your pocket.

If you desire customers, visualize the number and see them doing business with you.

If you desire things, visualize the kind of thing you want and see yourself with it.

If you desire a position, visualize the kind and it will soon make its appearance in your experience.

4. Relax, meditate, and be positive when you visualize your desire.

5. Be aware that ideas are infinite and the ways to manifest them are as uncountable as the stars of the heaven. Make your selection.

6. Engender a feeling of kindness into your desire. It sends out vibrations of love that are the source of attraction.

7. Thank God for the abundance that is yours now. Repeat daily.

8. Remember—an idea based on good backed by a sincere desire and held to by faith never fails to materialize.

The Law of Wealth is ideas on the job.

Decide now to be the master of your affairs, the director of your ability, the conductor of positive thoughts, the doer of good, and the captain of your activities. Hold fast to these tenets with dogged determination, unflinching courage, and unfaltering faith. Remember, every element in the Universe is here at your command to help you satisfy and realize your desire. Draw on these forces. Create a plan, reach out for the thing you desire mentally, and in that spirit of gratitude claim it as a reality. "Believe that you receive, and you shall have them."

The full power and strength of the Mississippi River is where it flows into the Gulf of Mexico. It is made up of many individual tributaries, and each one contributes its share to converge into one great stream of power and strength.

You are like this great river. You are made up of many tributary attributes and qualities, and each one contributes its individual share to make up your ability. The full power and strength of your ability is to converge these individual tributaries. Each chapter in this book aims to develop your individual qualities and attributes and to converge them into one great stream of power and strength. Read, study, and apply the contents of each chapter. They will put this power and strength in action and help you turn your ability into cash.

But don't take forever to get started.

Do it now!

Chapter 2

TAKE A TIP FROM "OL' MAN RIVER"

A minute ago I suggested a parallel between the Mississippi and man . . . between the Father of Waters and you.

Now, let us go to Niagara Falls for a moment and consider the famous Blondin who crossed, year after year, those perilous rapids on a tightrope. How he did it nobody knows, but Elbert Hubbard, a famous journalist of that day, put a finger on one cogent reason for his repeated triumphs on a wire over Niagara: "Blondin's feat in crossing Niagara on a tightrope consists of not stopping to think about it."

Take all the time you like to mature and perfect your plans, but don't take forever to make a beginning, once you've made up your mind.

The Mississippi doesn't hang around its source daydreaming of a distant objective, but starts moving and gathering power and strength each successive mile on its long and tortuous journey to the Gulf of Mexico.

Its message has been set to song.

"Ol' Man River just keeps rolling along!"

There is no more important word in the idiom of success than *action*.

When Demosthenes was asked what the first part of oratory

11

was, he answered, "Action"; and what the second was, he replied, "Action"; and the third, he still answered, "Action."

More men have been cheated of their destiny by inaction than by any other cause. And even men of mediocre talents have achieved success beyond their dreams by the simple process of harnessing great energies to modest abilities.

For action itself is a form of ability, and the greatest talents are useless without the decision and the drive to launch them and put them over among those we are anxious to reach and impress.

You will find the word "action" frequently repeated in these pages, but it is important enough to deserve a chapter to itself, since action is one of the most important phases of a successful life and an imperative command for the man who wants to convert his ability into cash.

I thought, at first, that I would reserve this chapter for the end of the book, and then it suddenly dawned on me that I was in danger of making the common mistake of postponing to the end a subject which, in any enterprise, properly belongs at the beginning.

The time for action is NOW!

Action wins wars, sells goods, pays dividends, solves labor troubles, stabilizes industry and government, and commands the grudging respect of men everywhere who are incapacitated and defeated by the inability to act. The earth is overrun with men who have something constructive to contribute to their tasks, but who lack the initiative to set their ideas in motion and to give momentum to dreams bogged down in complacency and inertia.

How often, in envy of another man's success, have you said to yourself, "He's got nothing that I haven't got"; or even, "He hasn't got as much"? Yet, far from being immodest, your conclusions may be demonstrably true; but only demonstration can prove it; and that's something the other fellow has that you haven't got! They demonstrate while others dream.

Many men, conscious of limited talents, are impelled to strike out and excel in a desperate bid for recognition, which explains why so many men of mediocre merit achieve distinction while better men are lulled into inaction by their advantages. It is no accident when second-rate men are acclaimed and first-rate men are neglected. It usually means that the man with only a second-rate talent has a first-rate gift for exploiting it.

The truth is, action must be an integral part of your equipment, or your other qualifications, however exceptional, will receive scant consideration in the market place. The world is on the side of the man who bestirs himself, and reserves its richest rewards for those who propitiate the gods for small mercies. If you possess the gift of action, you need not fret too much about your limited endowments.

There is an even better word than action; it is so closely identified with that admirable quality that it may be called the better part of action. That word is audacity.

Danton in the Revolution cried out for "De l'audace, et encore de l'audace, et toujours de l'audace!"

Audacity—still audacity—always audacity!

Fortune favors the bold.

Do not think, however, that I advocate a lack of caution in your bid for the laurel. On the contrary, nothing is more important to your success than to review and to remedy your weak points in advance of the test and to guard your deficiencies against surprise. Be bold but beware. I simply want to point out how often courage succeeds where caution fails. You need both, of course, but keep in mind that the man who strikes fares better than the man who hesitates.

And so, we come back to the headline of this chapter, "Take a Tip from 'Ol' Man River.' "

Just keep rolling along!

Chapter 3

ARE YOU NINE-TENTHS UNDER WATER?

Man is not the largest physical creature in the world, yet he has dominion over the earth, and all things in it. God gave this dominion to man through Mind and the conscious ability to form ideas. The capacity to form ideas gave man the ability to reason. The activity of reason gave man the power to control. Through control man became the Master. Since he is the Master and has this control, he should exercise his intelligence to establish dominion over himself, and not act as an accident in the world.

On the wings of his imagination, man is able to fly around, and make an investigation of things both material and immaterial. He flies around among the planets in the solar system, stars in the different stellar systems, and even makes a speculative investigation of the Universe, and his relationship to it.

His intellect is capable of reviewing himself and his own achievements, and also of contemplating the cause and source of his own creation. Man, through his imagination and acquired knowledge, discovers and explores the physical laws, and harnesses these laws and puts them in service for his comfort and convenience. With his vast capacity to know and to understand,

15

Man fails to turn the spotlight on himself. He gets acquainted with everything but himself. This he leaves to the "isms," "ics," "ties," "ious," and permits ignorance and superstition to control them. Once man applies the same knowledge and science to himself that he applies to physical things, human misery and poverty will be a thing of the past.

Don't Forget the Man

In the so-called busy world the tendency is to lose sight of the individual man. Most of us are thing-minded and lose sight of the man in the thing. Everything that man creates has its origin in Mind. It is an invisible idea before it is a tangible thing. It is a thought, then a product. The ability is Mind in action to create, invent and build all things.

Speaking of losing sight of the individual man reminds me of the time when the Professor of Astronomy at the University of Virginia was showing me through the Astronomical Observatory. In this observatory were charts, maps, globes, atlases, pictures, and diagrams, portraying a complete and comprehensive panorama of our solar system, and other stellar systems. In describing the infinite magnitude of these great systems, the Professor turned to me and said: "And to think of all these worlds upon worlds without end, and their infinite magnitude, and then to compare them to the little thing we call 'man.'"

"Yes," I said, "Professor, that's true, but do not forget or lose sight of the fact that the astronomer is still a 'little man.'"

He looked at me and said: "Mr. Prevette, that is an excellent observation and I thank you for it."

Man is the joint heir to a Consciousness that is common to all men. It furnishes the means and supplies the method through which ideas are communicated, otherwise it would be impossible for us to understand each other. This Consciousness is infinite, ideas are inexhaustible, and the ability to harness the two is limited only by its own estimation.

Is Your Ability Under Water?

What is ability? Ability is the capacity to act, the quality or state of being able. It is the power to perform, whether physical, moral, intellectual or legal.

The ability of the average man may be compared to an iceberg: about nine-tenths of it is under water. Professor William James, the eminent and renowned psychologist, estimated that the average man uses only 10 per cent of his real ability, while the other 90 per cent is latent. Latent ability is potential power, and can be released by the proper encouragement and the proper treatment. The might and power of ability feeds on its own achievement, and when inspired it permeates the whole consciousness with a synchronized responsiveness and any art, craft, or business is performed efficiently, and enjoyed freely. A superior service is rendered and a larger income is earned.

How to Develop Your Ability

The first way to develop ability is application.

Ability cannot be developed all at once. It is like building a house. One brick must be laid at a time. Most people want to begin with the house instead of with the bricks. Things are not built as a whole, but in parts, and each part must be built. The same principle applies to ability. You must build a little each day. Suppose that you develop three sentences each day on the improvement of yourself, a profession, craft, or business. At the end of one year you will have a total of eleven hundred sentences, and at the end of four years enough material for a book. This can be accomplished in fifteen minutes each day. A little built each day is amazing in its results.

The ability of man is versatile. One year his ability expressed in labor and art is transforming material into implements of destruction. The next year, using the same kind of material and the same ability with a change of method, he is transforming material into implements of comfort. Either of these performances requires an application of ability. Application turns the ability toward the transformation of some material into a useful service, or to illustrate some idea in the form of a plan. The precious fruit of application ripens in the mind itself to establish an experience, wherein idleness and vague, uncertain tendencies prevail. The ability enlightens and enlarges itself through its own application.

A party of explorers was driven by a storm from the Amazon River far out into the Atlantic Ocean. They had no fresh water aboard, and for days they drifted, suffering untold agony from thirst. They almost perished for the lack of fresh water.

To the great delight of all aboard, a ship finally hove in sight. They signaled it frantically to come near, and asked for fresh water. The captain signaled back: "Let down your buckets. There is fresh water all around you."

The explorers were not aware that the Amazon River remains fresh more than a hundred miles out to sea. These men were drifting in a body of fresh water and were almost perishing from thirst. Many people are like these explorers. In the midst of plenty, a world overflowing with abundance, they are begging for opportunities. Opportunities are as plentiful as the air. They are all around you. Let down your buckets and draw on that inexhaustible ocean of latent ability.

Application

The application of what you know reveals many things you do not know. "But as it is written, eye hath not seen, nor ear heard, neither have entered into the heart of man, the things which God hath prepared for them that love Him." Application puts this principle of the Bible in operation. Application of ability is like steam to a locomotive. It draws into action all the mechanism and channels it into power.

Challenge

The second way to develop ability is to lay down a Challenge.

In analyzing those individuals who have made a phenomenal success, we find that it was not the result of elaborate education, or of specialized training. On the contrary, most of these individuals had little formal education and none of them was trained for leadership. What is the secret behind such phenomenal success? These individuals had one quality in common —the daring ability to start something. They challenged their own ability. They dared to think for themselves. They determined to do something and to rely on their own. With confidence engendered by action, they drew on their own ability to do things others thought impossible. They did not know they could not do it, so they went ahead and did it.

In preparing this book, I was challenged. My wife and children dared me to write it. I thought it was an opportunity to share a few ideas with others. I accepted the challenge, and even though my field is not journalism, here is the book in its second edition.

Pasteur, who gave more knowledge for the preservation of health than any other man, was not a physician. Whitney, the man who invented the cotton gin, was a school teacher in Connecticut, far away from the fields of cotton. John D. Rockefeller was a clerk in a produce house. Andrew Carnegie was a bobbin boy. Thomas A. Edison was a newsboy. Henry Ford was an electrical mechanic. Benjamin Franklin was a printer's apprentice. Morse of telegraphic fame was a portrait painter. Bell, the inventor of the telephone, was a teacher of sound. Eastman, the Kodak king, was a bank clerk.

Men who blaze new trails, charter new routes, pioneer new methods, make new discoveries, and invent new things are men who dare to do things that can't be done. While others falter, they go forward. Seek, search, and things shall be revealed, even the innermost things of perfection. A man does not need pull. He needs to think. A challenge to dare, an incentive to undertake, and an urge to begin turns most things into a blessing. He who dares to think stands secure in the majesty of his own might.

Organization

The third way to develop ability is to Organize.

Ability is personal and only you can develop it. Only you can raise all or a part of the hidden nine-tenths. Organize your present qualities and attributes. Be fair, but strict. Be true to yourself and you cannot be false to others.

The following pattern is a suggestion for organization:

Put down on paper a list of all your past achievements, regardless of their importance. Analyze each one and try to visualize improvement. A review of past performances conjures courage to attempt other projects. Some of your best achievements have been spontaneous with little or no preparation. This may be a clue to your real power, and an incentive to develop your natural talents.

Make a list of your personal attributes and qualities. It may assist you to answer the following questions: What is my attitude toward myself, toward people, toward God, toward my neighbor, and toward my job? Do I think and act positively? Am I tolerant and considerate to other people? Do I honestly respect the rights and opinions of others? Do I interrupt while others are speaking? Do I tell my affairs to everyone I meet? Do I practice the Golden Rule? Do I permit the whims and fancies of misfortune to deter real issues? Do I realize that little issues may be big ones? Do I monopolize the conversation with a big "I" and a little "you"? Am I arrogant and impudent? Am I honest with myself? Am I persistent and progressive, without being offensive? Am I blown around from opinion to opinion, like a thistle in a wind-storm? Do I cultivate habits that make me strong physically, mentally, and spiritually? Do I have confidence in my ability? Do I dare to think for myself? Do I dread to act? Do I hesitate, falter, postpone, and procrastinate? Do I like to co-operate with others? Do I indulge in gossip? Do I like to work alone? Do I practice the little acts of courtesy in my daily associations? Do I remember to say: "Thank you," "Pardon me," "Forgive me," "I'm sorry," "Excuse me, please," and others? Am I willing to live, love, and share? Do I covet what others have? Am I envious? Am I jealous? Do I pray and work against selfishness? Conscious attention to the improvement of personal qualities and attributes improves the social and business relationship of any individual and if indulged in, they will distinguish him.

Make a list of your specialized knowledge. In what field are you most proficient? What business offers you the greatest stimulation? Can you lose yourself in what you are doing? Can you present ideas in a scientific plan? Can you make an intelligent blueprint of your personal qualifications? Are you versatile? Can you tell wheat from chaff? Do you have a new interest in your job? Do you exercise your imagination? Do you challenge your own ability? Do you read each day something to provoke thought? Do you cultivate your sense of humor?

Intelligence is the capacity and ability to size up yourself, size up your environment and to organize them into a workable plan that you may share life's abundance.

Freedom

Ability is seeking self-expression and functions more efficiently when the mind is not loaded down with a lot of false and specious importations. All kinds of rumors, hearsays, dreads, superstitions, and dire speculations are constantly infesting the air. Ninety-nine per cent of these mental vagabonds have no leg on which to stand. They are only fantastic phantoms to harass, subdue, and delay the ability's action. Here are a few examples: "Have you heard this one?" "Don't tell anyone I said so . . ." "Confidentially speaking . . ." "During my last operation . . ." "Have you heard about so and so?" "Between you and me . . ." "I don't seem to be able to get started." "The trouble with the world is . . ." "My situation is different . . ." "This is a good one . . ." So they travel *ad infinitum*. The moment any of these mental vagabonds cross your path, do not stop them, let them keep going.

"Old Pop Judgment" and "Old Mom Advice" are on every corner to tell you how to do it, or to advise that it is impossible. Then there is Cousin Tom, Dick or Harry with a wet blanket to dampen the spirit. Each one has a brand of expert knowledge. How can anyone know the value of your ideas when they have had no part in creating them? Take suggestions, but let the dictates of your judgment be the final word. Everything in the Universe is organized. Organization is the secret of scientific development and fruition. It gets rid of excess baggage, and permits the ability to function with freedom.

Vision

The fifth way to develop ability is Vision.

Most people believe only in the things they see. Appearance is everything. To attribute power to appearance is superstitious. Appearance is only a manifestation and has no power in itself. All power is invisible. Mind is invisible. Wind is invisible. Sound is invisible. Life is invisible. Spirit is invisible. Electricity is invisible. Put two wires side by side, charge one with a hundred thousand volts of electricity, let the other one remain inert, and you cannot distinguish between them. The only thing visible about electricity is the manifestation of light. If you doubt that electricity exists, touch a live wire.

Vision is something seen otherwise than by ordinary sight. It is a visual image of a plan in action. It is peeping through the fence of appearance. To believe in things you can see is sight. To believe in things you cannot see is vision. When vision fails, men perish. Vision is the camera of the imagination, and supplies the film to register the image.

For thousands of years the Niagara River dashed over the rocky cliff, and was only an interesting sight for visitors. A wise man, with a vision, recognized its great potentialities. Why not convert this great force into power? Today those falls have not changed, but the invisible power concealed in them is turning the wheels of a thousand industries, and supplying electrical power to light and heat thousands of homes. By drawing on his latent ability, the man with a vision harnessed the power of countless horses and converted it into a useful channel to serve his fellow men.

Vision is one of the most important faculties. It develops foresight and turns hindsight into profit. Every man has a portion. Use it.

Co-ordination

Ideas have a kinship and form excellent partnerships to produce harmony. When this kinship is recognized it illuminates and invigorates the ability. When ideas conflict, distraction confuses and disrupts the ability. It is unable to function with full force to reach its goal, or to enjoy a complete fruition.

Listen to that which is good and object to that which is defeatist.

Special machinery is constructed to perform specific jobs. A knitting machine makes hosiery. A lawn mower cuts grass. Both machines are excellent performers and do a splendid job in their respective fields. However, it would entail a severe conflict to attempt to mow a lawn with a knitting machine or to knit hosiery with a lawn mower. The same principle applies to ability. My ability has been developed in the field of human relations, and regardless of how good this ability is, it would be thwarted and confused in the field of obstetrics. The field of human relations, and also the field of obstetrics, are not crowded with perfection, and each field offers the ability a lifetime of interest and investigation.

A host of ideas is seeking a partnership to improve and perfect your occupation. To be co-operative, effective, and beneficial, these ideas must be regulated and expressed through co-ordination. Therefore, stick to one field, and as the ability develops in that field, the field enlarges and the ability expands. Let harmonious ideas co-ordinate and feed your ability, and your ability will feed you.

Conviction

Every day Parson Jones visited his church to preach. Someone asked him why he preached six days each week to himself,

and only one day each week to his congregation. His answer was: "It takes six days of preaching to convince myself, and only one day to convince my congregation."

One of the most difficult jobs is to convince ourselves, but once this is accomplished it is fairly easy to convince others.

Simply remember that half-baked dough is not bread.

Conviction comes from two Latin words, "con," and "vincere," which means "to conquer." In order to conquer doubt about your ability to perform, either by argument or belief, it is imperative that the proposition be thought through to a conclusion. Half-baked conclusions are the result of faulty reasoning. Thinking through can only reach one conclusion—the proposition is either true or false. If it is true, make a decision with conviction, and act upon it with determination. A state of being convinced is predicated upon the integrity of the human mind. When fed with facts, the mind does not err and the decision reached inspires conviction.

To realize the full impetus of ability and to derive the full benefit from it, a thorough and wholehearted conviction must permeate and embrace every phase of your occupation. The occupation must warrant this, otherwise the standard must be raised, or a new field of endeavor sought to allow full expression.

In my forty years of experience in the field of selling, I have always acted as my first customer. My conviction has been if it is good enough for me to buy, it is good enough for me to sell. On the other hand, if it is not good enough for me to buy, it is not good enough for me to sell. Acting on this conviction, success followed.

Conviction based upon the principle of good is invincible and never fails to convince. It puts the ability in operation in high gear. It acts with confidence and determination. Convince yourself, and you convince all others. A few strong impulses, a little

gumption, a rule or two, and a dose of conviction, and the ability goes into action.

Before closing the book on this chapter, I suggest that you read, review, and study each one of these seven ways and think of them in terms of your own ability. As a definite reminder, I will list them.

1. *Application*
2. *Challenge*
3. *Organize*
4. *Freedom*
5. *Vision*
6. *Co-ordination*
7. *Conviction*

God is not partial to a fortunate few. His unlimited gifts and riches are free to all. However, there are certain laws that govern them.

How You Can Overcome Obstacles

During World War II, many stories were told of how man faced and overcame what seemed to be insurmountable problems and conditions. When faced with a crisis, hidden powers come to man's rescue—his own and the power of God! He finds himself doing the impossible and performing so-called miracles. The exigency of the situation provokes means to solve it. Latent ability does not seek a favorable occasion to work. It is instantaneously available for any occasion and will work for any one at any time. It is not necessary to get in a foxhole or to be stranded at sea to find God's Laws. The great epic of the Pacific was Rickenbacker and not a rubber boat. Miraculous achievements become commonplace once man learns to draw on his latent

powers. A miracle is only a fulfillment of one of God's Laws which man learns to understand and apply.

Electricity turns the inert electric bulb into a shining light. Gasoline vapors turn a motor into action, and steam turns a locomotive into a vehicle of energy and power. At this very moment, your ability can revitalize and remake you. It turns negative thinking into positive action. It turns pessimism and despair into hope and confidence. It turns dissipation and defeat into application and progress. It turns all effort into health, happiness, and achievement.

Fairy tales are founded upon wisdom and mysticism. When you learn to draw upon the invisible Laws of God, and use your ability to apply them, many more fairy tales will be a dream fulfilled.

Your ability is the product of your thoughts. Be satisfied with none but the best. Remember: and your dreams shall benefit accordingly.

Chapter 4

CONVICTION, LIKE CHARITY, BEGINS AT HOME

In the previous chapter I enumerated seven keys to develop ability. I should like, in this chapter, to expand the seventh.

I said that the seventh way to develop ability is conviction. It is also the only way to prove ability. Without conviction, the abilities perish.

How Conviction Gives You Power

You can't get anyone to believe in you unless you believe in yourself. You must be convinced, yourself, before you can convince me. It is for you to set the pattern of my belief.

So powerful is this influence of one man's conviction in himself that it is often sufficient to promote a wrong idea. This, in fact, is the secret of the 'confidence' racket all over the world.

A 'confidence' man knows that his mission is false. But he has the same conviction as a man whose mission is true: he believes that he can put it over. And conviction, unfortunately, is just as effective in a bad cause as in a good one. A man's conviction may be genuine, though his intentions are not.

But don't let these remarks beguile you from the path of virtue. I merely want to make the point that the more strongly you believe in yourself, the easier it is for you to command the

28

belief of others. You and I simply cannot overemphasize the tremendous importance of conviction in telling our story to those we are anxious to impress.

How to Express Your Conviction to Others

Conviction is a gift. It is the white flame of a personal evangelism. But it is no good unless it is articulate. Many a man, rightly convinced of his abilities, is defeated because he is deficient in the really very simple art of revealing and promoting his advantage. His convictions are without contact and no man can succeed if nobody knows the facts about him but himself. Convictions begin within, but they must demonstrate themselves on the outside, or they are useless for practical, profitable purposes.

Obviously, the convictions of an inventor are manifest in his invention. The first Ford car, the Mazda lamp, the Singer sewing machine, and a thousand other great inventions each spoke for the man who thought it out and put it together. There was no need for rhetoric. The argument presents itself in visible, tangible form. But, with most men, whose faith in themselves is an abstraction without the support of concrete or tangible evidence, the convictions are another matter. They must be orally and forcibly expressed.

A man must know how to speak up and to convey his inner excitement to his audience. This, however, does not require him to have a glib and facile speech. On the contrary, that very quality may be inconsistent with the story he has to tell and the impression he is anxious to create. A simple but terrible earnestness is a more persuasive argument than a flow of words. Be brief and sincere and let the truth and the merit of your convictions do the rest. It is enough to feel deeply and to let your listener sense the restraint behind your spoken words.

We are all familiar with the phrase: a burning conviction. This phrase admirably expresses what a deep conviction is. It is something that burns within and grows gradually into a steady and inextinguishable flame. But we know how we can use it to light up for us and others the way to better things. Different men have different means of communication. A poet, a statesman, an industrialist express themselves, respectively, through the medium of prophecy, promise, and product. The poet is preoccupied with the dreams of a people; the statesman is concerned with the demands of a people; the industrialist is occupied with the needs of a people. And each succeeds in proportion to the strength and the constancy of his convictions.

How to Strengthen Your Convictions

But it is a mistake to think that this evolutionary process applies only to a special breed of men. It is available to all of us. It applies to all of us. Indeed, it is more operative among those who are most in need of it and whose limitations give impetus to the resolve to succeed. The less you have, the more room you have to expand. Modern America is a monument to men who rose from nothing and who converted their abilities into a driving wedge of conviction that they had something unusual to offer in their own particular sphere of activity.

Now at this point it is the custom of an author to fortify his argument with big names in American business and industry. That is just the thing I don't want to do. I don't want to do it because it has been done to death. The names I want to cite are obscure and unknown. They are the names of men who hesitate to cash in on their convictions and who stand irresolute in the wings of a stage that is waiting and eager for their wares.

There are men in every field of endeavor who lack the courage of their convictions. They have labored long and hard to improve their talents and skills and are to-day equipped to invade the higher echelons of command. But they have more timidity than temerity. They pause on the threshold of hopes ready to be fulfilled and waste in indecision their just rewards.

Your convictions are the sum total and the salvation of all your hidden abilities, and once you put them into action, place and power will accrue to you from those who are in a position to promote you.

Chapter 5

HOW TO INCREASE YOUR OWN POWER TO THINK AND TO BUILD

You sprang from a cell, a cell invisible to the naked eye. This cell had the power within to think and to build and to do it in harmony with law and order. It used mathematics to determine the number of things necessary to make up your body. It used chemistry to determine the chemical properties necessary to nourish your body. It used physics to determine the energy necessary for your body. In logical sequence, this cell drew on the forces of life and through the division and the multiplication of other cells, built into orderly arrangement a human body. When completed its reward is a birth certificate.

At birth, five sense avenues were available to sponsor thinking. Eyes to see, ears to hear, nose to smell, tongue to taste, and touch to feel. To use these sense avenues, it was necessary to think. The accumulation of these sensations developed impressions. These impressions turn into knowledge. Perception was formed. You were aware of things. You could distinguish objects and recognize sound. You had the ability to know and the capacity to gain knowledge.

One day along the line memory dawned. You discovered the ability to recall events, remember names and faces, and to retain information and knowledge. You had the capacity to observe, to concentrate, to remember, and to reason. You were a rational creature, able to censor and discipline your own acts. You were aware of yourself and conscious of your own identity. Who am I? Where did I come from? Why am I here? You were seeking the cause of things. What was their origin? What was back of them? You were able to comprehend the invisible idea back of the visible thing. You could see the man in the vase, the artist in the picture, and the thought in the product. You were acquiring the ability to form ideas, to establish the relationship between cause and effect, and to have a conception of your own ability. You were beginning to understand. You were conscious of your power to think. Today that cell has developed into a human personality, and with the power to think is reviewing its own inception, its own development, its own ability and its own advancement.

This plan of development is the one that human beings follow normally. It proves that man is a thinking creature. It is a normal and natural attribute to think. From the moment of conception, a man is a thinking creature. In his early development, he followed certain definite laws of thinking in a natural way. The ability to be conscious of these laws should be an added incentive and an added inspiration to believe in them, to demonstrate and apply them in all activity. By adhering to the principle that he is a thinking creature, man can come to a complete fruition of his power to think and to build.

I believe it was Plato who said: "There is nothing great in the world except man, and there is nothing great in man except Mind." The capacity of the mind to think is based on certain laws. There are five of these laws, and an understanding of them will give you the power to think and to build. The application of these laws will help to turn your ability into cash.

1. How to Use The Law of Observation

Man's first teacher was his eyes. He opened his eyes and marveled at the things he saw. By constant vigilance he discovered
he had not only an eye to see, but also a brain to interpret. He
began to observe the things about him. He marveled at their
existence. He noted the many changes in nature and the repetition of the four seasons. He observed the sun and the moon and
noted their various changes. He recorded these observations.
They were passed along from generation to generation as basic
knowledge. Thus civilization was developed with its vast store
of information, facts, science and knowledge. Most of our books
are a recorded experience based on observation and interpreted
in relation to other basic knowledge.

What is observation? Observation is the act or faculty of
observing or taking notice. It is the act of seeing or fixing the
mind upon anything. It comes from the Latin word "observare,"
which means "to save," "preserve" or "keep."

The world is a panorama of passing events. It is crowded
with people, things, words and manifestations of nature. Each
one affords an ample opportunity for observation and study.
Take advantage of your surroundings, observe your environment, and make what you observe a part of your knowledge.

Observation is the best teacher to develop the social graces.
It teaches courtesy, which is the act of being thoughtful and
considerate of others. It teaches you not to walk in front of
someone without saying "pardon me." It teaches you not to
forget to say "thank you" when someone holds the door open for
you. It makes courtesy count much in your life.

Observation teaches you to observe things in nature. A good
part of my understanding has been gained by observing the

sun, the moon, stars, clouds and the infinite variety of natural things. They all teach and enrich our capacity to think.

The other evening going out to Chestnut Hill on the train, I glanced through the car window. A beautiful sunset was beginning. I dropped the paper instantly. I began to observe the sunset. Before me was nature in all her glory. Hue melting into hue, translucent blue and rose, and the palest green lighted with golden gleams and flecks of regal purple all adorned the sky. Its majesty, its beauty, its magnitude filled me with awe and respect. It aroused in me a love and admiration akin to reverence that only such beauty can bring. It was a mental feast. It inspired my consciousness with greater appreciation and a more profound understanding. It made me think.

Observation broadens the outlook, enlarges the perspective, gives depth to understanding, sharpens the wit, and makes you more responsive to opportunities.

Ruskin said: "The commonest things in the world are the most worth while." Observation trains you to see the little things, and to realize that all big things are made up of a lot of little things. Anyone can see the boulders, but it is the little pebbles that throw you. Try to see a thing in all its component parts. Observe its form, size, and color. It will instruct you to compare. To compare is to analyze and to analyze is to think.

The inspiration and enthusiasm to invent, the inclination to make new discoveries, and the desire to improve any existing plan or thing are the result of observation.

Thomas A. Edison said: "I usually begin where others leave off. Through observation and my own knowledge I am inspired to keep on." Edison learned from observation that electricity would produce light if properly resisted in a highly sensitized coil. He found the answer in the tungsten coil to produce the famous Mazda bulb. In all, Edison patented over twelve hundred items, and most of them started with observation.

James Watt sat in his mother's kitchen and observed the agitated lid of a boiling kettle. "Steam has power. I will harness it," he said. The steam engine was the result.

Charles Goodyear observed the mixture boiling on the cook stove. It overflowed and congealed into an elastic mass. From this observation he discovered rubber.

Charles F. Kettering, president of the General Motors Research Corporation, was down on the farm visiting his mother. She was still using the old-fashioned oil lamps. By observing the lamp, an idea to invent the Delco System came to him. Today, as the result of that observation, thousands of farmers enjoy better lighted homes.

The first bed was a hole in a cave. The next man put leaves in the hole. The next man put some twigs under the leaves. The next man made a cot. The next man put legs on the cot. Finally man put springs and mattress on the cot. Today, as a result of observation, you enjoy a bed.

The same principle applies to the development of transportation. First it was the wheel. The wheel turned into a cart, the cart turned into a wagon, the wagon turned into an automobile, and the automobile turned into an airplane. The whole process was based on observation.

Thus you see the value of observation to increase your power to think. Try to get fun and pleasure from the things you see. You will pick up many valuable ideas. This breeds interests and starts you on the road to creative thinking. Creative thinking will make you rich in both material and spiritual things. Train your eyes to see, and train your mind to interpret. They will teach you to think and to build.

2. How to Use the Law of Concentration

Did you ever stand on the bank of a river and watch the water as it whirled around a center or vortex in the stream? Did you observe how that vortex or center drew to itself everything that came floating down on the current? That was an active, positive center, distinct from any other center or vortex in that stream, and because of its individualized strength it had the power of attraction, and everything was drawn into it.

When you concentrate your mental forces you become the vortex or center of intelligence, and you can draw to yourself anything that you desire.

What is concentration? Concentration comes from the Latin word "concentrum," which means "to center." It is directing the mind to a common center. It is paying strict attention to the job at hand. It is holding the mind on any subject to the exclusion of all others. It is the directing force which hastens to the materialization of your desires.

Like observation, you must have a specific subject on which to concentrate. This must be people, things, words or ideas. Concentration is a positive and creative condition of the mind.

How to concentrate through listening

One aid that will help you to concentrate is to train yourself to listen. Man could understand sounds and could communicate with his fellow man long before he developed the art to read and write. He depended on sound signals. Ears are the means to record sound signals, and to develop the ability to listen. Nature gave man two ears and one mouth. He is supposed to listen twice as much as he talks, otherwise he would have two mouths and one ear. Do not be too eager to impress others with what you say, but be eager to hear what they say. Keep your ears open and your mouth closed. It will help you to concentrate and let you in on many valuable situations.

A Serbian shepherd boy, minding his flock, stuck the blade of his knife into the ground of a pasture. He struck the blade and some other shepherd boys resting on the ground many feet away heard the sound signals. This gave the Serbian shepherd boy an idea. Twenty-five years later, this boy, Michael Pupin, by using the principle of ground signals, made it possible to talk across the continent by the telephone. He kept his ear tuned to the ground.

How to concentrate through reading

Another aid to help you to develop the power to concentrate is reading.

Napoleon once said: "Show me a family of readers, and I will show you a family that rules the world."

Good books are the brick and mortar that hold civilization together. They keep alive the past and they also enliven the present.

What is a book? It is what someone has seen, felt, imagined, experienced, or discovered, expressed in words to convey to you this knowledge and information. Therefore, by reading you come in contact with the great minds of the past and of the present. You learn to comprehend with Shakespeare, to reason with Plato, to meditate with Emerson, to observe with Burroughs, to weigh and to concentrate with Bacon, to think with Socrates, to share Lincoln's compassion, to feel the stir and the drama of Churchill, and generally to profit spiritually from minds deeper and broader than your own.

I do not presume to tell you or any other man what books to read specifically. That is something that your own taste must determine. In your diet, you eat what you like and abstain from what you don't like. The same is true of books. One type of book will appeal to you and another will not. The all-important thing is to be interested in books. Books themselves will form your taste if you form the habit of reading them. But I want to make one suggestion with which I am sure you will agree. Read books that interest you and not because it is considered correct to read them. If the classics are too heavy for you, forget them. If the philosophers bore you, dismiss them. If great poetry leaves you cold, leave it alone. If great novels fall short of your expectations, there are ten thousand others at your beck and call. Read for the joy of reading and not to conform to vicarious acclaim. Meanwhile, remember that good reading broadens the appreciation of all literature and almost surely you will turn later to authors who seem a little remote to you now.

Reading makes a full man. It is a yardstick for comparison, a leveler for understanding, a square for sizing up, and a plumb rule for concentration. It provokes thought, inspires meditation, engenders reflection, aids deliberation, and gives you greater power to concentrate on the job. It increases your understanding, gives you an insight into the thinking of others. It helps you to form a pattern of thought and will help you to influence and motivate others to think and act. It helps you to analyze and visualize. You learn to think around, and through, things. It opens up new vistas, ripens judgment, stabilizes thought, and teaches you to be tolerant and considerate of others. It helps you to grow and expand.

Some years ago a group of well-known businessmen from New York were fishing off the coast of Florida. They were favorably impressed with the unusual display of knowledge and information by the old captain. The fact that he was so well read, so well versed and so well informed led these men to believe that he must have a very valuable and extensive library. Their curiosity amused the old captain. He invited them to his home to see his library. They went. They found the old captain in his cabin reading by the light of a candle. They were astounded as well as amused. They asked to see his library. The old captain put his arm under his coat and pulled out an old, well-worn book, torn from use and brown with age. It was an *Old Blue Book Speller* (the kind that had everything in it but the kitchen sink). The old captain was proud of this book. With a smile on his face and a twinkle in his eye, he proudly displayed it and said: "Gentlemen, this is my library." The old captain knew accurately and thoroughly everything in that book. That knowledge distinguished him. He acquired it by applying the Law of Concentration.

The late William Lyon Phelps, one of America's foremost educators, urged everyone to read and to concentrate on the Bible as a means to a liberal education. He said: "I thoroughly believe in a university education, for both men and women, but I believe a knowledge of the Bible, with a college course, is more valuable than a college course without the Bible. For in the Bible we have profound thought beautifully expressed; we have the nature of boys and girls, of men and women, more accurately charted than in the work of any modern novelist or playwright. You can learn more about human nature by reading the Bible than by living in New York." This is a splendid tip on how to develop the Power of Concentration.

As you read, pick out key words. Get the full meaning of these words well established in your mind. Use them as pegs on which to hang other thoughts. In this way a full pattern of thought is formed in your consciousness and you can remember what you read, and make it a part of your knowledge.

I never concentrate for a long period of time on one subject.

Thirty or forty minutes is sufficient. When it gets boring, it is time to relax. The best way to concentrate is to read three or four books in one evening. Read forty minutes at one time in each one. The change of subject matter stimulates new brain cells, and instills zest and enthusiasm. In following this suggestion you can read for two hours without great exertion. You can concentrate and retain what you read.

How to concentrate on every-day details

Another good aid to concentration is to form the habit of concentrating your thoughts upon everything you do in your daily life. I am an insurance broker. I do most of my selling by telephone, so I always carry a pocketful of nickels and dimes. When the hunch strikes, I immediately call my man. I give him the plan. I focus my ability. I arrest his attention. I incite his interest. I concentrate. I do not wait to call him next week, next day, or next hour. I call him instantly. The way to do the job is now. Hit the iron while you are hot. I have made many substantial sales following out this suggestion.

Whatever you do, concentrate. When you tie your shoe, tie your shoe, do not try to read the paper. When you shave, shave, do not mow the lawn. By concentrating, I shave in less than two minutes.

Another aid to help you concentrate is found in the newspapers. Word puzzles, anagrams, letter-out schemes, vocabularies, test your facts, bridge hands, twistagrams, and many other items of interest can be used successfully to help you concentrate.

Put down the word Procrastination. By using only letters that make up this word, see how many everyday English words of four or more letters you can make from it in twenty minutes. It is an excellent game to help you concentrate. Try it.

A good clue to develop concentration is to select something you like. Centering your interest and attention on one subject trains you to undertake other things. This feeling of accomplishment invigorates and encourages you.

Concentration may be compared to swimming. You probably learned to swim in shallow water, without knowing that you were doing so. When you got in deep water you could exercise that ability. Concentrate on the little things, and the big ones will take care of themselves.

Exercise your power to concentrate and you improve your power to think and to build.

3. How to Use the Law of Memory

You never forget what you remember. You forget because you forget to remember. Any fact, knowledge, thing, event, experience, word or plan once imbedded into your consciousness becomes a part of you. You never forget it. There is no trick to memory. It is using your power to observe and concentrate.

Memory comes from "memor" which means "mindful." It is to be mindful of the thing you want to remember. It is the power or function of reproducing, and identifying what has been learned or experienced. The function of remembering. The function of memory includes learning, retention, recall, recognition, and sometimes it includes certain habits and skill.

To memorize a thing by rote is one of the quickest ways to forget it. Memory is more than memorizing. It is the strength and trustworthiness of your power to re-present or recall the past with authority.

You can train your memory. Age, education or environment do not enter into it. You have all the qualities and attributes now, otherwise you would not be reading this book. Here are five suggestions that you will find practical and helpful.

Aids to help you remember

Analyze what you want to remember. Take it apart, and put it together. You think in terms of words, and you remember in terms of words. A word names a thing. It may name a person, a subject, a plan, a number, a thing, or an idea. The word and the thing form a partnership in your mind. This association makes it easy for you to remember. Therefore, concentrate on what you want to remember, analyze it, and tie it together with words. In doing so, you never forget it.

There are five key words in this chapter. They are observation, concentration, memory, reason, and action. Analyze these words and think of them in terms to improve your power to think and to build, and you will remember the contents of this chapter.

Therefore, analyze words, get their full meaning, incorporate them into a sentence, and use them in your conversation. In this way words become your property and you can turn them into cash.

Be accurate. The late Joseph Pulitzer, one of the greatest publishers of all time, had over his desk in bold letters one word—Accuracy.

Ask three people for the same information and in all probability you will get three different answers. Information or knowledge is either accurate or inaccurate. The effort expended to get inaccurate information is greater than the effort expended to get accurate information. Accurate information speaks for itself; inaccurate information must be explained. Accurate information is permanent. Inaccurate information must be checked.

Facts, events, dates, numbers, names, and knowledge do not

change. They are fixed, and to fix them accurately in your mind is to remember them.

Why do you remember the multiplication table? Because the knowledge is accurate and you only had to remember it once.

Why do you remember July 4, 1776? It is accurate knowledge and this date occurred only once.

The same principle applies to names and faces. My name is Earl Prevette. I have had that name for nearly sixty years and if I live another sixty years it will still be my name. It is only necessary to remember my name once, and you have it always. By considering people's names in this way, you take interest in the name, you get it accurately and you remember it.

In dealing with people's names be accurate. Get the name correctly. A person's name is a symbol—a trade-mark, a badge that distinguishes and identifies that person from one hundred and fifty million other persons in the United States. A person likes his name. It individualizes and sets him apart. He likes to see it in print and he likes to hear it spoken, but he wants it accurate.

A name is a perfect symbol. My name is Earl Prevette. That name is a perfect symbol. One letter in the wrong place makes it imperfect. Therefore, when someone addresses me as Carl Private, he tells me something. He tells me that he is not interested enough in me to get my name accurately. Naturally, I feel if he is careless about a little thing like getting my name accurately, he might be careless about other things. Certainly he might fail to get the consideration due him. The reaction of others may be the same.

By all means get names, facts, numbers, knowledge, and all information accurately. It will not only help you remember, but it will add to your power to think.

Visualize. Create a mental picture of what you want to remember. Put into this picture all parts of the things you desire to retain, and tie these parts together with words. Concentrate on these words, study their relation, use them as pegs on which to hang other correlative information, and register them on the film of the imagination.

Sometime ago I saw a hunting picture. I visualized what I saw. Even now I can see the wide-open fields, the alert dogs, the well-groomed horse, and the smartly tailored hunter in his red jacket with cap to match. To tell you about this I use words. It is necessary to name things and only words can do it.

Idealize. To idealize a thing you take it into your consciousness, associate it with other ideas, expressed in words, and actually feel it in action. When you visualize, you see all the parts of a thing. When you idealize, you not only see all the parts of a thing, but you actually feel them in action.

When you idealize the hunting scene, you can feel the ground under your feet, you can see the dogs leaping, hear them barking, you can see the horse galloping and hear the hunter's horn.

To idealize information you feel yourself not only recalling it, but re-presenting it in detail. Idealize your activities. It is a marvelous method of rehearsing and perfecting your act. It eliminates mistakes, prevents blunders, increases efficiency, and takes the sting and worry out of your job. Idealize your errands and a string around your finger to remind you is unnecessary.

Review. By all means review the things you want to remember. Do not just repeat them. Analyze them, be sure they are accurate, visualize them, idealize them, and dramatize them into action. It will surprise you how many things you can review and recall in a few moments. You can review your favorite poem, quotation, Bible verse, bridge hand, day's activity, sales plan, interview, appointment, or any other special knowledge while taking a bath, riding in a train, waiting for an appointment, or just sitting around. Try it; it is a stimulant and a tonic to the mind and body. It keeps the information fresh and keeps you prepared.

4. How to Use the Law of Reason

Solomon, one of the wisest men that ever lived, said: "He that is slow to anger, is better than the mighty; and he that ruleth his spirit than he that taketh a city." God gave man the power to reason and by exercising it man has complete dominion over his thoughts.

What is reason? Reason comes from the Latin word "ratus," which means "to reckon," "believe," or "think." Reason is the power to think straight. It is plumbing the bottom, and getting at the root of things. It is the ability to comprehend all the factors and arrive at a sound conclusion. It is the capacity to arrange facts and knowledge in logical sequence. Mortar holds the bricks together and reason holds the thoughts together. Reason based on common sense is a practical and an efficient method to do things effectively.

To demonstrate the Law of Reason, I approached a group of railroad presidents by letter on the subject of "How to Sell by Telephone." The first impression is, how can railroad companies use a book on selling by telephone?

Reason has a different story. Reason says that railroad presidents are interested in good ideas, otherwise they would not be railroad presidents. Reason says that these men are busy and to make the letter brief, concise and to the point. Therefore, 1 cut a three-page letter down to six sentences.

This letter gives Mr. Fairman an idea, tells him how to make use of it, and supplies the means to do it.

This plain letter got 80 per cent favorable response.

Mr. Donald Fairman, *President*
U and M Railroad Company
10 Wall Street, New York, N. Y.
Dear Mr. Fairman:

Thousands of telephone calls come in and go out from your company each year.

Thousands of opportunities to sow seeds of good will, build prestige, and improve business.

Make each telephone call count.

How?

By using: "How to Sell by Telephone." It is an efficient means to make every telephone call count, and get results quickly.

Get a copy of this book for each key man and watch the business roll in. I am,

Sincerely yours,

Earl Prevette

Following out the Law of Reason, the following sales plan was developed on life insurance. It has sold millions of dollars' worth of life insurance.

The plan

First: This Plan creates for you and your family an Estate immediately. This Estate, Mr. Doe, is unlike most Estates. It never depreciates in value, and is always worth one hundred cents on the dollar. This Estate is free of all liens, mortgages and liabilities. This Estate can be administered for your family so as to be exempt from certain types of taxation.

Second: This Plan establishes a savings account for you after the second year. A very valuable feature about this savings account to you, Mr. Doe, is that it is always available. It stands at your elbow ready at a moment's notice to furnish you with ready cash to cover any unforeseen contingencies, or meet any emergencies that might arise.

Third: This Plan pays all future deposits for you in the event you should become totally disabled through any kind of disease or accident. This guarantees your Estate, and keeps your savings intact.

Fourth: This Plan makes it possible for you, Mr. Doe, to retire with an income for life at any age between fifty and sixty-five. This income will be guaranteed to you as long as you live with absolute assurance that every dollar invested in the Plan will be returned to you or to your beneficiaries.

This Sales Plan has approximately two hundred words and gives a compound idea of the benefits of life insurance. It is a true and concise statement of fact. It does not attempt to define life insurance with its many technical terms. On the other hand, it presents a very comprehensive picture of what life insurance will do for the prospect and his family; and does it in a very understandable way. It is spoken in his language and he understands it. He quickly senses that this Plan is an opportunity to do some real things for himself and family. In doing this, and by taking on the Plan, he feels he will be adding to this happiness and to his family's welfare.

This Sales Plan puts the Law of Reason into action.

In applying for a position, follow this pattern of reason. Give your name, address, telephone number, date of birth, height, weight, health and dependents. Put this information at the top of the page. Follow through with information about education—high school, college, and special training. State summer school activities. State extra-curricular activities and sports. State experience and any specialized training. Tell what you can do, and visualize what you are capable of doing.

Others only know what you tell them. Follow the Law of Reason and you can tell them intelligently and effectively.

In applying the Law of Reason to your affairs, you will be unlike the salesman who talks for 15 minutes to the prospect, only to have him say: "Well, I do not know what you are selling, but I will take one."

Let the Law of Reason stand sentinel over your thoughts, permit it to establish equilibrium in your life and what you do will be done with a purpose. An ounce of reason saves a pound of energy, and also a pint of ink.

5. *How to Use the Law of Action*

In the City of Bagdad lived Hakeem, the Wise One. People from all over the country went to him for counsel and advice. He gave it freely, asking nothing in return.

There came to him a young man who had spent much, but got little for his money. He said to Hakeem: "Tell me, Wise One, what shall I do to receive the most for that which I spend?" Hakeem answered: "Anything bought or sold has no value, unless it contains that which cannot be bought or sold. Look for the Priceless Ingredient."

"But what is this Priceless Ingredient?" asked the young man.

Spoke then the Wise One: "My son, the Priceless Ingredient of every product in the market place is the Honor and Integrity of him who makes it. Consider his name before you buy."

Action comes from the Latin word "agere" which means "to do." It is the application of what you know to what you do. Between the two is a middleman. The middleman is character. Character is the spirit of honor and integrity that you put into that which you do. It is the spirit to be your best and do your best at all times. It is a desire to see the job well done.

It goes back to Elbert Hubbard's mousetrap. Build a better one and people will beat a path to your door. Put the right spirit into your job, and people will seek you out. It magnetizes your efforts. People want to do business with you.

It may be a service you want to render. It may be a product that you want to market. It may be a plan to improve some business. Whatever it is, remember that people have the same inherent qualities, and what will appeal to one will appeal to the other. They are motivated by thoughts and ideas. Mix with these the Priceless Ingredient. People like it. It establishes your value. The Law of Action is made efficient by doing the job well.

In this chapter I have given you five definite laws on how to think and to build. Go back and review each one, and get the spirit of its meaning. They will help you. As a reminder, I will list them.

First: The Law of Observation.
Second: The Law of Concentration.
Third: The Law of Memory.
Fourth: The Law of Reason.
Fifth: The Law of Action.

Everything is a product of thought. You think, then build. The quality of thought determines the quality to build. Compare an Indian adobe to a modern dwelling house.

You have the power to create thought forces. Thought forces revealing your qualities mixed with the Priceless Ingredient built into your plan of action are a vital, living force, the most irresistible force in business. These thought forces give your plan of action color, form, essence, substance, and the spirit of power and dynamic impetus. They define and clarify your product or service with simplicity. They establish a meaning and make others feel about your product or service the way you feel. They carry a message of fact. They persuade and convince.

They bring home the bacon. They turn your ability into cash.
As Joseph Addison wrote in one of his plays, a long time ago:

> 'Tis not in mortals to command success,
> But we'll do more, Sempronius,
> We'll deserve it.

Chapter 6

JUST WHAT IS THE SECRET
OF POWER?

The Greeks have a word for it and it still remains the best answer after thousands of years.

Knowledge is Power.

That phrase has been repeated so interminably over the centuries that today it is a cliché, which as you doubtless know, is a stereotyped expression for an obvious truth. But that does not detract from its value in the philosophy of life. We do not destroy a temple by flinging bricks through the window. When the violence abates, the temple stands.

The Greeks were right and so is the man who listens to their counsel.

I have discussed at length in Chapter 3 the high value of enthusiasm in any activity and I mean every word of it. But a few reservations are necessary. "Do the thing and you shall have the power" is true. It is also true that power itself generates enthusiasm. I simply want to make the point that enthusiasm alone cannot take the place of power.

Let me put it another way. We think of a good salesman as a man who can talk. But the best salesman is the man who knows what he is talking about. That is power. Knowledge of the King's English is a great asset, but knowledge of your sub-

52

JUST WHAT IS THE SECRET OF POWER?   53

ject precedes it in importance. One helps the other, but the second comes first in impressing your audience. Know your stuff and the rest will follow. Enthusiasm carries contagion—it is catching. Power carries conviction—its message registers and its import remains.

So, we come to the secret of power, and the ancient Greeks and all human experience are in accord.

The secret is Knowledge.

How Knowledge Can Give You Power

Over the years I have met many successful men in all walks of life, and one thing has always impressed me. They were so saturated with their subject, whatever it happened to be, that usually it was the subject that did the talking rather than the speaker. The voice was the medium of expression, but you couldn't hear the voice for the story, so intense was the conviction behind it.

While lecturing on art on one occasion, in London, James McNeill Whistler, the celebrated American artist, was thus interrupted by one of his audience:

"But a minute ago, Mr. Whistler, you were arguing . . ."

"I beg your pardon," flashed Whistler, "I am not arguing, I am telling you!"

Another authentic Whistler story is appropriate to this chapter. In the case of Whistler *v.* Ruskin, growing out of Ruskin's scornful comment on Whistler's now famous 'Nocturne in Black and Gold,' for which he had asked two hundred guineas, Sir John Holker, Attorney General presiding, asked:

"How long did it take you to knock off that 'Nocturne'?"

"I beg your pardon," said the witness.

Sir John apologized for his flippancy.

Chapter 7

LEARN TO SPECIALIZE

Josh Billings, a very popular American humorist in the last century, said this:

"Konsider the postage stamp, my son—its usefulness konsists in its ability to stick to one thing till it gets there."

Why It Pays to Specialize

Specialization is frowned on in some quarters and applauded in others, but the affirmative side has the better of the argument. To do one thing well in a world where so many things are done indifferently surely says more for specialization than against it.

It may be true that a fanatical absorption in one subject to the total exclusion of others is unfavorable to a well-rounded individuality. It is also the secret of a well-developed individuality in its chosen activity. It is, of course, the nature of fanaticism to resist the intrusion of outside interests. A fanatic works in one medium. That's what makes him a fanatic. It is also what makes him efficient and successful. A man cannot be well-grounded in one thing and well-rounded in all.

Nobody derides specialization in the artist; such criticism is reserved for the businessman. Yet what man is so completely self-centred and engrossed in his work as the artist who pours his heart into a painting or a poem? His work and his reputation are the fruit of an undivided devotion to one object and one objective. And it is so in business. Every successful businessman is an artist in his allegiance to what he sets out to do. He may sometimes carry it too far, but that is better than not far enough. No man can be a specialist and a varietist at the same time.

How to Be a Specialist

Choose your objective and let nothing interfere with it. Do not dissipate your talents and your energies on side issues that contribute nothing but impediment to your progress. Hew to the line. Make up your mind that this is an age of specialization and that the man who excels in one line of endeavor has taken the first and most important step in the direction of success. Don't let outside interests compete with your main purpose. You're going to have competition enough from others without developing it in your own orbit. Stick to the script.

The late S. Clay Williams, President of the R. J. Reynolds Company, was once listening to an advertising agency group soliciting the Camel account. When the discussion turned to the subject of copy, the spokesman for the agency proudly proclaimed what he thought was an overwhelming reply.

"We have forty copy writers!"

"How about two good ones?" asked Mr. Williams.

That was even more overwhelming!

Stereotypes come in bundles; stars don't. And stars are everywhere in command at the top or in the higher echelons of executive management. They are also in constant need of new recruits, as they move up or are tempted elsewhere by better offers. It is a fallacy that there is no room at the top. It is the lower rungs of the ladder that are crowded. And, of course, it is on the lower rungs that special talents and skills must first seek to assert themselves.

Learn the Rules for Specialization

The specialist is no exception to the rules of apprenticeship. He must serve his time at humble tasks before he can advance to higher responsibilities. But even in the performance of these tasks, he must begin to develop and display those qualities that will enable him to climb.

And now let us ask ourselves a question.

Just what is a specialist?

We live in an age of "high-falutin" terms and phrases, and sometimes the definitions of progress obscure rather than clarify and explain it. Obviously, a specialist is a man who specializes in one phase of a subject: a physician preoccupied with one detail of the anatomy; an architect absorbed in one type of construction; a lawyer committed to one branch of the law. But specialization, in its broadest interpretation, goes much deeper than that.

How about the clerical drudge who keeps books, for example, the disillusioned salesman who solicits a hostile world for orders, or all the other minor and neglected figures in the industrial economy? What hope does specialization hold for a man caught in the vise of a restricted or a distasteful activity? If he likes the nature of his work, specialization will enable him to expand its scope and importance: if he doesn't like it, specialization will open the door to something else and something better.

Above all, specialization is the spirit with which a man approaches and apprehends the hidden opportunities in the work before him. It is the ability to bring new vision to a routine task. It is a challenge to his capacity for growth.

"Seest thou a man diligent in his business? He shall stand before kings."

Remember the warning of the poet:

"A favorite has no friend."

So, let's look into the problem of getting along with others.

Chapter 8

HOW TO COPE WITH YOUR ENEMIES

How to get on with people is called public relations.

How to cope with your enemies is even more important.

It is a law of evolution running through all nature that opposition, even enmity, is conducive to development and growth.

How to meet opposition and convert it to his advantage is the mark of a diplomat in his relations with others.

Cede an inch and cinch a mile!

There is nothing so disarming as a policy of conciliation in placating envy and malice.

Very few men can endure the humiliation of being eclipsed by another man in the same organization, who, they feel, has no more ability than themselves.

And the man who can rise above his fellows without making them resentful of his success does what most successful men are unable to do in any capacity.

In fact, generally speaking, men do not resent another man's success so much as the arrogance that usually goes with it. They are repelled by his superior airs.

A Story of Kindness

Many years ago, Charles M. Schwab, President of the Steel Trust, told the story of two plant executives whose long standing friendship had been disrupted by one man's forging far ahead of the other. Years of confidence and intimacy were succeeded by mutual contempt. They no longer spoke, no longer even passed the time of day. The cleavage was complete, and Schwab heard about it. He also knew that neither man liked it, so one day he suggested to the successful one that he go to his old friend and patch up their differences, and the man said:

"Why should I? Why doesn't he come to me?"

"Because," said Schwab, "your success has probably changed you a little—it changes everybody—and the gesture will come better from you."

The suggestion worked, and an old friendship was renewed.

I think one of the finest examples of handling an enemy intelligently and magnanimously is the one I am about to recite.

Although it occurred fifteen years ago, the principals are still alive and active in the same industry, though no longer in the same company. The company in which the little drama took place is an important subsidiary of a great chemical corporation, and at the time of which I write, it was also the background for an intensely personal feud between two men. Let us call them "A" and "B." "A" was executive vice-president and "B" was only a notch below him in authority. From all that I could learn at the time, "A" had repeatedly offered the olive branch to his rival but to no avail. "B" was eaten up with envy and jealousy; and although there was no open break between them, they remained unreconciled.

Meanwhile "A" had become president and "B" had taken over the duties of executive vice-president. It was thus that matters stood some months later when a situation arose that revealed a sharp contrast of character. You shall judge which was the better man.

The parent company needed a man to build up another sub-

sidiary and the choice, temporarily, favored an outsider. "B"
very much wanted the job, but obviously his hands were tied.
If his candidacy were known it might expose him to summary
action by his superior, to whom, of course, he could hardly
look for sympathy or support. But time was pressing, so he
decided to speak to him, anyway.

If he were an applicant for the job and failed to get it, how
would that affect his present relations?

"Wouldn't change them at all," said the president, "though
I hope you don't get it. You're a very valuable man in this out-
fit and I'd hate to lose you."

"B" was too overcome with astonishment to say anything
but "Thank you." He was even more embarrassed on his way
out, when his quondam enemy called him back and said:

"Eddie, if I can do anything to help, let me know."

Eddie could hardly believe his ears. It surprised him to discover kindness where he had never looked for it. But he wel-
comed the offer, for his superior stood high in the councils of
the parent company.

"I'd appreciate it," he said, "if it's not too late."

"I'll get busy right away," said the president.

A week later Eddie secured the appointment and today the
two men are fast friends, though the little man will never be
the equal of the man who repaid meanness with kindness.

How to Overcome Enmity

Jealousy and malice are active ingredients in every business
organization in America. Wherever you look you will find one
man filled with enmity toward another, and the other probably
similarly afflicted. It is seldom that animosity is one-sided.
But, as a general rule, the aggressor is less competent than his
victim. The most frequent cause of conflict between two men is

the envy that proceeds from a disparity of talents. Men are not, ordinarily, jealous of their mental equals; that is the tribute they pay to their superiors. Nor is this contemptible quality confined to the more lowly walks of life. It is the curse of both commoners and kings. Small men swarm in high places, and history records countless examples of men whose secret hates would disgrace a fishwife.

Senators in Rome were jealous of Caesar; they killed him. Men high in the government were jealous of Lincoln; they reviled him. Officers in his army were jealous of Washington, and one of them, General Charles Lee, betrayed him at the battle of Monmouth. Even Napoleon, who surely had no reason to be jealous of anybody, was so bitter against the man who defeated him at Waterloo, that he bequeathed, in a codicil to his will, a substantial sum of money to the man who would assassinate the Duke of Wellington!

The minute you start to go ahead, you incur the disfavor of the man behind. He can't help it. He regards your rise as a reproach. He is not filled with joy that the tide is turning your way; he resents the widening gap between his life and yours. There is only one effectual way to handle his resentment. Ignore it. Act as if you are unaware of it; and, above all, do not make matters worse by an ostentatious display of your advantages. That is one of the chief causes of one man's jealousy of another; not your progress but your airs. Be modest. If your success makes a difference in him, take care that it makes no difference in you. That is the best answer you can give to the man who resents any success but his own.

Chapter 9

HOW TO DOUBLE YOUR ENERGY

There is a secret in "How to Double Your Energy," and I believe that I have discovered it. In my opinion, it may be accomplished by applying the principle suggested by Shakespeare over three hundred years ago. " 'Tis the mind that makes the body rich." This is a profound and scientific statement. It reveals a most valuable idea, and my purpose in this chapter is to develop this idea fully and to share its complete significance with you.

People are interested in having more energy, but they are absolutely callous, indifferent, and adverse to the old system of calisthenics. They remember too well the tortures of setting-up exercises, weight-lifting exercises, daily dozens, dumbbell exercises and a lot of other weary and uninteresting procedures. Thinking of it, to say nothing of attempting it, makes most people cringe with dread and writhe with a tired and weary feeling. My sympathies are with them.

Shakespeare gave me a clue to a new system of calisthenics. I felt that you would like to know the secret of how to make the body rich in health, vitality, strength, vigor, endurance, and energy and how to eliminate all the old antiquated methods of exercise that have been in vogue since the first cave man pounded his chest and shouted: "Look who I am!" Therefore, using myself as an example, and my own body as a guinea pig, I have evolved a system of calisthenics based upon the science and practice of free bodily exercise without apparatus to promote strength, gracefulness and energy. This system uses your head as well as your muscles. It involves no tricks or magic, and requires no hours of drilling or other wearisome exercises. It eliminates body torture, stiff muscles and tired feelings. You can successfully put this system into practice in the home, in the office, on the street, in the automobile or any other place you might happen to be. It only takes a little thought and a couple of minutes each day. But the results are phenomenal.

It has always been my contention that no one has a right to offer, to suggest, to propose, or to advance any theory on how to do something, especially if it influences others to try it, either directly or indirectly, unless the person advancing that theory has used it, and finds through actual practice that it will do all that is claimed for it. My song is: "Practice what you preach"; otherwise theories are not worth the paper on which they are written. This system to double your energy may appear to you to be a theory. It is a theory, but one that I have learned from actual experience. Every suggestion advanced has been practiced and demonstrated by me. I have lived each and every one of them. I know their value. What they are doing for me they can do for you. Learn and apply. Study and use. Fathom the secrets of your marvelously constructed body, and care for it scientifically. These secrets will teach you to live with zest and joy. They will double your energy.

The body is the house in which we live. It is the temple of the spirit. It is the source of all energy. It is the organ of activity. However, the body itself does not create energy. This is the function of the vital organs within the body. Energy is created through the process of these organs making and distributing blood. Blood is life. In the blood lies your strength and energy. As a self-propelling, self-sustaining, and self-acting organ, the body lives and thrives on blood. Blood is the source of energy.

God created everything and God is good. The infinite variety of things expressed in nature proves that we are surrounded with an Infinite Intelligence and Power that establishes law and order in the universe and supplies us with all the essential material elements necessary for our well-being. As individuals we enjoy the right to draw on these elements and God has endowed us with a mind to make a wise use of them to meet our personal needs.

"Blessed are they which do hunger and thirst after righteousness, for they shall be filled." Happy are they that make the "right-use-ness" of the elements, for they will be filled with pure blood and dynamic energy.

The four best-known material elements used by the body to make blood are Air, Food, Water, and Sunshine. The wisdom used to assemble these four life-making elements determines the quality of blood that makes the body rich.

Nature provides man with all the elements necessary to make steel. Man applies mind in making the proper use of these elements. In doing so he is able to make the finest and toughest steel.

Let us discuss and analyze the four elements that make pure blood.

How to Get the Most from the Air You Breathe

When you were born, the first thing you did was to breathe in air. Nature provided you with lungs with which to do this.

It is estimated by science that the average person uses only about fifty per cent of his lung capacity. The other fifty per cent lies idle. Nature is not extravagant in her gifts, and usually portions things out as they should be used. The blood needs oxygen, and one way to obtain it is through air. The function of the lungs is to supply this need, but with fifty per cent capacity idle, there is a possibility that the blood may be suffering for the want of oxygen. Therefore, the first suggestion is to make complete use of your lungs. Train yourself to breathe deeply and fully. It is following out a natural law. Make it a habit to consciously breathe deeply and fully once every hour during the day. In doing this you exercise and expand the lungs, help to purify the blood and enlarge the diaphragm. Conscious deep breathing also aids relaxation. Always remember that the forces in the air are vital and living. They help grow and sustain every form of life. The blood needs it and the body will suffocate without it. This air is free. Breathe it. It will help to reenergize the entire body.

How to Gain from Food

The second element you cried for upon your arrival in the world was food. The body must have food in order for the blood to have nutrition.

What is food? Food is the different things we eat. It is a product of the earth, air, water, and sun. These elements make and supply the food with vitamins. "Vitamin" comes from the Latin word "vita," which means "life." Vitamins are life-giving forces found in the natural state of foods. They are essential for proper nutrition.

How does this life-giving force get into the body? Through the blood stream. This action is accomplished by a manufacturing and distributing process carried on by the internal organs. Food is taken into the mouth, chewed, swallowed, then digested by the stomach and made ready for the small intestines. The small intestines, through the process of osmosis, pick out the particles of food that contain vitamins. These particles are turned over to the vital organs, including the liver, heart, lungs, kidneys and others; and each one of these working in harmony with the others converts these particles into blood, and distributes this blood over the body to supply the cells with nutrition. Thus you have life, heat, and energy.

There is only one conscious act on your part in the whole process of converting food into blood. That act is mastication, which is to chew, crush, and grind the food with the teeth until it becomes a pulp. The fact that this is a conscious act makes it one of the most important acts connected with food. It is another proof: " 'Tis the mind that makes the body rich."

To prove the great value of mastication, put a piece of stale unbuttered bread into your mouth and chew it long enough to produce a digestible liquid. The indeterminate taste at the beginning now tastes almost as sweet as sugar. Thorough mastication of this piece of bread gives the saliva digestive power by stimulating the constant outpouring of the enzymes, which help to turn starch into sugar. When this pulpy mass reaches the stomach, it is partly digested and the stomach can do a much better job. This applies to everything you eat. By thorough mastication the stomach can digest every particle of food. The conscious preparation of it through mastication means less work, and less wear and tear on all the other internal organs that manufacture the blood. It frees you from indigestion and other distressed feelings, and supplies you with richer blood, which produces better health and more energy.

As an insurance broker, I had an occasion to approach a man to buy life insurance. He stated that he was uninsurable owing to high blood pressure. He was a strong, vigorous type of individual, and I felt that I had a clue to his condition. I invited him to lunch. He ordered a very substantial meal and in almost less time than it takes to tell it, the entire meal had disappeared. I asked him if he made it a habit to eat his meals quickly and to bolt his food. He replied that he had never even thought of it. I suggested for his own health, happiness, and peace of mind that he practice the principles advocated in this chapter, and two months later the high blood pressure had subsided. Search for the cause of the ailment, and you will discover the remedy.

Natural laws are man's best teacher, and the observing of these laws reveals the truth. In connection with the importance of mastication I want to call your attention to the cow. Did it ever occur to you that a cow must eat sufficient food to maintain her own large body, and at the same time give several gallons of milk each day, furnishing us with all our valuable dairy products? The cow has a secret. She chews her cud. The herbaceous food is swallowed unchewed, and passes into the rumen, whence it is regurgitated in masses. Then it is thoroughly masticated and mixed with saliva while the animal is at rest. Thus, without mastication, there would possibly be no milk, no butter or cheese.

That suit which you have on is also a product of thorough mastication. The sheep is also a ruminant animal that chews its cud. This is why it is possible to have wool for woolen clothes. Sheep are maintained to grow wool just as long as they graze and chew their cud. When their teeth wear out, they are sold for mutton. That's the reason the people in England get tough mutton chops. The sheep in Australia have worn their teeth out grazing and chewing their cud while producing wool. Hence they are sold to England for mutton.

Most birds and fowls swallow their food without chewing it. Nature was kind to them, and gave them gizzards. The gizzard chews and masticates the food for the birds and the fowls. Nature was also kind to you. She gave you a mouth and a set of teeth with which to chew and masticate your food.

The value of mastication was demonstrated when you were a baby. Only once in your life did you double your body weight in one year. That was between the time that you were born and your first birthday. That, too, has a secret. All your food was liquid and did not require mastication.

A furnace will burn better and furnish more heat one-half full of coal than it will choked full. Overloading the furnace smothers the flame, and a large portion of your heat is lost. The same principle applies to the stomach. When it is overloaded with food, much of the value is lost because the stomach is using up energy in digesting it. This induces sluggishness and tiredness. Thorough mastication prevents this because the more thoroughly food is digested, the less is needed. It is not what you eat, it is what you digest. When the cells of the body are properly nourished it is not inclined toward obesity, nor does it suffer from underweight.

The cellular mass in the marrow of the bones secretes red blood cells, and this mass is fed by the food you digest. Thorough mastication of your food helps to feed this cellular mass, and this enriches the blood. This releases more vibrant energy to more cells, and makes the body glow with health and vitality.

Take plenty of time to eat your meals, practice mastication, and remember that the time saved bolting food is lost a hundred ways in health, energy, enjoyment, efficiency, and peace of mind.

How Water Can Make the Body Rich

The third element to make the body rich is water. Three-fourths of the earth's surface is water. More than three-fourths of your body is water. This reveals another clue: furnish the body with plenty of water. The body demands water at all times. The atmosphere around us is continually absorbing water from the body. It must be replenished, or the body will suffer from the lack of it. Water is essential to furnish the body with sufficient moisture to keep the pores of the skin open. This helps the body to get rid of toxins and other waste matter. The only way to have plenty of moisture in the body is to keep it well supplied with water.

Give a wilted flower or a half-dead plant a drink of water, and observe how quickly and completely it revives. The water seems to stimulate all the other life-sustaining elements. This holds true for the human body.

The kidneys are the organs that help to make and purify the blood. They need water. Water is a cleansing agent used by the kidneys. It helps to dissolve all the poisons and impurities out of the blood. When the blood is pure, it flows more easily and nourishes and restores the cells more quickly. Blood is the life-giving force of the body. A free flow of it revitalizes, rehabilitates and rebuilds every fiber, every cell, and every muscle of the body. When the cells tingle with pure red blood, your body functions with vibrant health and glowing energy.

You take an external bath every morning. Why not try an internal bath? Drink two tumblers of water when you first get out of bed. It will possibly make you feel a little squeamish at first. If it does—that's a good reason why you should drink it. The squeamish feeling is a warning of toxins and the water is helping to get rid of them.

Don't wilt up, and don't dry up. Keep your skin young and glowing with health. Water helps. Train yourself to drink two tumblers of water on rising, and drink at least one tumbler every two hours all through the day. It is nature's tonic. Drink it.

How to Benefit from Sunshine

The fourth element helping to make the body rich is sunshine. Did it ever occur to you that all the food you eat is either grown in the summertime or in the tropics? The rays of the sun are the answer. In the summertime, the rays of the sun are intensified because they strike the earth more directly. The intensification of the sun's rays accelerates the vibratory forces of the air, and these are capable of growing all kinds of foods and vegetation. This happens in the temperate zone during the summer months, but in the tropics or territory bordering on the tropics, it happens all through the year. In the tropics it is possible to grow food at any time. Spices are grown only in the tropics. They require the more intensified rays of the sun, which the temperate zone cannot provide.

All vegetation thrives in the sunshine, and so do we. The body needs it. A short sun bath, not to the point of burning the skin, taken two or three times each week in the summertime, is very beneficial to the body. The rays of the sun are vita-rays, which heat and charge the cells with vitamins. These vitamins are loaded with energy and the body absorbs this energy from the sun just as a blotter absorbs ink. These vita-rays taken in the summer will increase your resistance against colds in the winter. Train yourself to take a sun bath occasionally, and by all means get into the sunshine as much as possible. It is a gift from God, and is here to help you get more energy. Make use of it.

How to Use One Exercise for Longer Life and Greater Happiness

The body is a plastic, claylike assemblage of protoplasm made up of cells. These cells are kept alive and revitalized and re-energized by the blood. The principles just enumerated have shown us how to make the best possible use of the four essential elements necessary to make pure red blood. Now that we have the blood, what is the next step? The heart is the organ that pumps the blood to all parts of the body. The arteries carry the blood from the heart, and it is returned by way of the veins. This is nature's wonderful system of distributing the blood. However, " 'Tis the mind that makes the body rich," and there is a conscious act that will assist the heart in the distribution of blood. That conscious act by you enables each cell of the body to be fully nourished with pure red blood at all times.

What is this conscious act? Again, we take a lesson from nature. It is estimated by science that most animals live five to seven times their maturity age. According to the American Mortality Tables, the average age of man is 61.2 years. This is less than three times his maturity age. If man lived five to seven times his maturity age, he would live to be one hundred to one hundred and forty years old.

What do the animals do that most people fail to do? What is the answer? The animals must have a secret. By observing them and using my body as a guinea pig, I have adopted and practiced their secret.

That secret is Stretching.

The animal follows his natural instinct. How often have you observed the cat arching its back, the horse swaying its back, the lion extending its body, and the dog spreading its paws?

These body actions of animals are revealing something. They are setting an example. They are telling us to stretch our body. Stretching is the only form of exercise that animals adhere to strictly. Therefore, it must be the natural and reasonable exercise.

Stretching is nothing more than conscious tension. It is tensing the muscles of the body by an act of thought. In my own experience, I have practiced all kinds of exercises but I have come to the conclusion that stretching is the best and most natural of all. It is easy to do. No equipment of any kind is necessary. You can stretch consciously for about ten to twenty seconds, and if you make it a practice to do this you will increase your energy and pep. Make it a habit to stretch your arm muscles, leg muscles, back muscles, stomach muscles, hand muscles, neck muscles, and shoulder muscles. Try to stretch every muscle in your body from head to toe. In doing this, also exercise your common sense.

What does stretching or conscious tension do for the body? To stretch the muscles is to stretch the cells. To stretch the cells is to cause them to expand and break up, and this gives the pure blood a chance to flood and feed them. This helps to drive out all toxins, acids, poisons, or other impurities. When the cells are crying for blood the body feels tired and by stretching at intervals you furnish the cells with nutrition and this substitutes energy for tiredness. You will have more capacity to do things. In brief, it is giving the body a blood bath.

If the cells of the body are not fed with blood, they dry up. This is very evident in people when they grow old. The cells in their face begin to dry up for the lack of blood, and as the blood recedes, it is like the moving out of the tides and what we see are wrinkles, dried-up skins, and withered faces. This never happens when the cells of the face are properly nourished with blood through conscious tension.

Stretching the muscles permits the blood to flood, and to feed and cleanse the cells, and there is no opportunity for the vultures of impurities and disease to start their panic.

To illustrate the value of stretching, drop a sponge in a pail of water. Watch the sponge absorb the water. Take the sponge in your hand—squeeze it out tightly. Now drop it in again, and the same thing happens. This illustrates how the cells react to blood when you stretch the muscles.

There is no particular way to stretch. Each individual can work this out to suit his own disposition, time, and convenience. The main thing is to *do* it. This is the way I do it. I take a deep gulp of air right in my mouth, all my lungs can hold. I tense the body, stretch all parts, raise the diaphragm, and press down. This throws blood to my head, face, shoulders, back, legs, abdomen, and neck. Then I exhale through the nose. This takes fifteen seconds and does it make you relax! Try it. Do this when you first get out of bed in the morning and at least once every two or three hours during the day. The great value of it needs no proof. Do it, and it proves itself. If the bones crack, then you know you are stretching. Squeeze your hand tightly and watch how white it gets. The blood is squeezed out of it. Now relax and watch the blood flow back. That is what stretching does for your whole body.

How to Walk for Livelier Condition

Another beneficial exercise I enjoy is walking. The average city block is about one hundred and fifty yards. This is about twelve blocks to a mile. When I walk twelve blocks, which takes about fifteen or twenty minutes, I find that I have exercised my legs seventeen hundred and sixty times, because there are seventeen hundred and sixty yards in a mile, and each step covers about one yard. By all means train yourself to walk. It invigorates the body, stimulates the flow of blood, and provokes many brilliant ideas. Try it.

How to Establish Rhythmic Living

Before concluding this chapter, I want to call attention to the Rhythm of the body. All things in the universe, including the sun, stars, planets, moon, and earth, move in rhythm. If this were not so, it would be impossible to have harmony, and the universe would instantly go to pieces. Harmony establishes balance, and balance establishes harmony. Natural laws are inexorable. They never deviate, and work with precision. Your watch is now ticking away to keep up with the sun. The astronomer sets his watch by the sun, but the sun never sets by the astronomer's watch.

The heart beats in rhythm and the blood flows in rhythm. Man did not make the heart beat. He discovered by experience that the heart beats on an average of seventy-two times per minute. Man did not make blood pressure, he only discovered it by experience. The whole body responds to rhythm. Rhythm can be produced by balance.

How can you establish balance in your body? By body posture. It is very easy. This is how you do it. Draw your feet together. Draw the abdominal muscles in just as far as you can possibly get them—just a little more, please. Now exhale all the air (carbon dioxide) you possibly can from your lungs— a little more through your nose. Relax. Do it again. Hold this position for five seconds. What are you finding out? This conscious act raises the diaphragm, extends the muscles of the abdomen, thrusts the chest out, places the neck and the shoulders in the right position, makes the lungs hungry for a deep breath

of air, strengthens your spine, straightens your back, gives the
solar plexus a workout, establishes rhythm and balance, and
develops body posture. By practicing this a few times each day,
which takes only five seconds, you are going to draw in the
waistline, and throw out the lifeline. This act also gives the
internal organs more space, and they function without being
crowded. Body posture qualifies you to walk correctly, thus
taking the weight off the stomach and putting it on the hips,
where it should be. It also aids in the equal distribution of
blood, and all parts of the body share it alike. It tones up the
whole body and bids farewell to old man constipation with his
whole gang of enemies.

Look at Cock Robin, apparently never sick a day in his life.
There he stands, like a general, at perfect attention. The moral
is: "Look, learn, and live."

A survey of a hundred leading men will show one attribute
common to all of them—Energy.

Energy makes the difference between a boxcar and a locomotive. As an illustration, here side by side are two locomotives.
The finest that were ever built. Both have the same workman-
ship, the same equipment, and same potential horse power. Put
steam in one of the locomotives, and it will pull a string of box
cars across the continent. The other one stays put. It is nothing
more than a boxcar. Steam-energy makes the difference.

Disobey a natural law and you pay a penalty. Obey it and
you receive a blessing. All the principles suggested in this chapter are based on natural laws.

" 'Tis the mind that makes the body rich." Therefore, think
health and visualize and idealize with positive thoughts the kind
of body you want, and remember the legend of the Prince who
was born a hunchback. Every day the Prince stood before a per-

fect statue. He visualized and idealized what he saw. In time he straightened up and acquired a perfect body like the statue.

The principles and suggestions advanced in this chapter will not make you a Samson nor a Sandow with bulging muscles protruding from every limb, but by adopting and practicing them daily you will have a strong body full of health and overflowing with dynamic energy. You will have the vim, vigor, and vitality to do your job efficiently and to maintain a sustained effort. Practice these principles every day, and do it religiously. They will double your energy. They will give you the power to act, and turn your ability into cash.

Chapter 10

HOW TO TURN YOUR CASH INTO ABILITY

How to double your energy suggests to me a short chapter on the idea of how to double your money.

I mean how to double, redouble, and re-redouble your financial resources progressively and indefinitely.

How to turn your ability into cash will also show you, once you have got a foothold, *how to turn your cash into ability.*

I here refer to the accumulative talent that knows how to consolidate its gains and convert them into new accessions of profit.

Money makes money and your first small success will open up new avenues and opportunities for making more. That is how great corporations and great fortunes grow.

How to Increase Your Initial Gains

Making a profit in your initial venture is neither so difficult nor so exciting as progressing from profit to profit in subsequent efforts. It is not so difficult because you have something to work with. It is not so exciting because now you are gunning for bigger game.

Do not misunderstand that previous paragraph. First success is sweet. There is something about it that does not come again.

I simply want to make the point that there is a greater thrill in bagging a tiger than in shooting a jack rabbit.

But a tiger hunt is dangerous. The bigger the game, the bigger the risk. An important banker told me years ago that it was astounding how many men who succeed in getting a financial start, proceed to dissipate their original stake through a lack of caution.

Caution should be increased, not relaxed, as our responsibilities and resources overlap and grow. We should guard against the complacency induced by success and cultivate and exercise the utmost vigilance in our transactions. For, money is vulnerable and the more we have, the more we are subject to the envy and the wiles of those who covet it. But conserve and protect it and the opportunities for increasing it are manifold.

Large Returns from Small Investments

Nobody knows how many businesses, great and small, have been founded or enabled to survive by some man who had money available when another man needed it. One man's necessity is another man's opportunity. I know of a number of cases where even limited funds, which were available as ready cash, have enabled men to reap rewards out of all proportion to the sums involved. The man who needs financial assistance must meet the terms of the man who supplies it. That is one of the immutable laws of money, whether thousands or millions are at stake.

Some years ago a manufacturer in New York, whose business, then recently started, showed a great promise of success, but whose resources were inadequate to develop it, was in desperate need of $25,000. A man I know, who had worked and struggled for seven years to accumulate just that amount, made a deal that gave him one-third ownership. This share during the past six years has returned him $25,000 annually. Another acquaintance of mine put $15,000 into a small chain-store enterprise and in five years got his money back ten times over. And these are but two minor instances of the major role played by ready cash in the rescue of the man who is short of it.

"Watch the Basket"

Save your money and watch for opportunities to get it to work at a profit. Then continue to watch it for your protection. Be cautious in choosing your investments and vigilant in supervising them. Carnegie said: "Put all your eggs in one basket and watch the basket." Maybe that was good advice in his particular case because he was referring to steel, in which he was at the time America's most competent and powerful authority. He controlled the industry and could speak with knowledge and assurance. Personally, I recommend a little variety in the baskets, but in any event the second half of the warning still holds: "Watch the basket."

And meanwhile, do not be discouraged because at present you have little or nothing to put into the basket. The important thing is to make a beginning, and the best beginning is to cultivate and practice economy in small matters to prepare yourself for future financial responsibilities. The trouble with most of us is that, in our quest of great gains, we are prone to ignore, or neglect, the little things that so often lead on to fortune.

Many years ago, a small boy applied for a vacancy in a Paris bank. His services were not acceptable. On his way out of the bank he suddenly stopped and stooped to pick up something on the floor. The man who had just dismissed him, probably wondering if the boy had found something of value, called him back and questioned him. The boy took from the lapel of his coat about the simplest, and certainly the cheapest, commodity on earth: an ordinary pin! He had learned economy the hard way.

An impoverished home had taught him that even so small an item as a common pin was important in the struggle for survival. He was immediately hired and that was the beginning of a great financial career.

He became the famous French banker Lafitte.

Chapter 11

THE KEY TO A FORTUNE

"In the beginning was the Word, and the Word was with God, and the Word was God" (St. John 1:1).

God gave man the power to invent and create words. By the use of words man is able to identify and classify all things in nature, and also to communicate thoughts and ideas.

Words have a long and varied history. The growth and development of words are interwoven around the customs, laws, and traditions of the people who invented and created them.

It is possible that words had their inception with the Egyptians. The Hieroglyphics was the first method used to record characters, symbols, and signs. This crude knowledge, through a combination of written symbols and also a combination of spoken sounds over a long period of time, created the Tree of Languages. (Indo-European—5000 to 6000 B.C.)

This Tree of Languages was composed of six original languages (1) Persian, (2) Greek, (3) Russian, (4) Teutonic, from which sprang English, Dutch, German, and Scandinavian, (5) Latin, from which sprang Italian, French, and Spanish, and (6) Armenian. From these six original languages and their offspring originated all the words in the English language.

With over five thousand years, and all these different languages from which to pick, the English language today has approximately five hundred thousand words. Everyone has an inviolate interest in all these words. A word becomes the property of anyone who uses it. A headful of words is better than a pocketful of money. Money is only a temporary convenience. Words are a permanent asset. Money is usually lost or spent. It is gone, but words once acquired are tools that may be used over and over again. The more you use them, the more potent they become. They do not wear out and will last forever.

According to the latest census report, there are about one hundred and fifty million people in these United States. All these people are prospects for words. Words move and influence people to act. Science has found from experience that those who take the lead, and pick off the choice plums in business and social affairs, are those who have at their command a choice stock of words. A large stock of words gives a wide range of knowledge, and develops more tools with which to think.

A vocabulary is a stock of words used in a language, by a class or individual, or in any field of knowledge. A vocabulary may be compared to a department store. A department store can do more business than any other store because it has a larger variety of merchandise.

A person with a large vocabulary can influence more people about more things than a person with a limited vocabulary.

Words are one of your best friends. Standing at attention, they are ready to go to work for you at a moment's notice.

"Attention, please!" was the greatest command among the armed forces. Two words—but what power! "Attention, please!" "Words" are the command in this chapter.

How to Develop an Interest in Learning New Words

Is there a practical and interesting way to increase your word power? You can stimulate your own interest in words by studying their derivations, meaning, and also their application. As a matter of interest, let us observe the history and origin of a few words.

"Daisy" came from two old English words meaning "day's eye." The flower opened at dawn as if it were the eye of the day.

"Universe" comes from two Latin words, "unus," meaning "one," and "vertere" meaning "turn." "Universe" means that which is turned into one, combined into one whole. That which functions under one Law.

"Sandwich" (two slices of bread with meat, cheese, jelly or the like, between them): In the year 1740 John Montagu, the fourth Earl of Sandwich, was so busy at the gambling table he did not have time to stop for his meals. He ate his meat between slices of bread, thus the name sandwich.

"Town" (any collection of houses), comes from the Anglo-Saxon word "tun," which meant an enclosed place.

"Hieroglyphic" comes from two Greek words, "hieros," which means "sacred," and "glyphein," which means "to carve." Hieroglyphic means "a sacred carving."

"Democracy" (American form of government), comes from two Greek words. "Demos" means people and "kratos" means "to rule." Therefore, democracy means "people rule."

"Confidence" (trust), comes from the Latin word "con," meaning "with," and "fidere," "to trust." With trust, to have faith.

"Alert" (on the watch), comes from the French term "alerte," "on the lookout" or the "watch tower."

"Infant" comes from two Latin words, "in," which means "not," and "fari," "to speak." "Infant" means "one who cannot speak."

"Alphabet" (the letters or characters used in writing a language) has been formed from the first two letters of the Greek alphabet. "Alpha," meaning "A" and "Beta," meaning "B." Thus the A, B, C.

"Cereal" (a grain prepared for use as human food). This word comes from the Latin word "ceres." Ceres was the name of the Goddess of Grain.

"Etymology" (true knowledge of words). This is the subject we are studying at the moment. This word comes from two Greek words, "etymos," which means "true"—"real," and "logos," which means "knowledge." The true and real knowledge of words.

These twelve words illustrate the interest and fascination there are in studying and analyzing the history and derivation of words. By consulting a standard dictionary you can make an interesting and profitable study of the origin of words.

How Words Communicate Ideas

All ideas, according to Professor James, the celebrated psychologist, are instantly associated with words. Therefore, words play an important part in all business activities and social intercourse. It is very essential to use the proper ones. People will react more quickly and more favorably to word stimuli than they will to pictures or colors.

Since words play such an important part, it is only proper and fitting that we should pause for a moment to analyze them.

What is a word? A word is a name. It is a definite unit of intelligence. It is a symbol that means or signifies something. Without meaning, it is a noise or just a sound. With meaning, it is a complete unit of speech, which signifies and communicates an idea. It is being understood. Therefore, we employ words to build a durable structure of communication.

Ideas and thoughts are communicated in two ways, oral and written. To make these two methods more vivid and elastic, words are incorporated in the different parts of speech. The noun is used to name a thing. The verb is used to affirm or to predicate something. It is also used to express action or mode of being. The adjective is used to describe. Words are the language to express our ideas, to make our message understood, our report clear, our deeds appreciated, and to carry on our social and business relationships with each other. Words discern and beautify our relations.

A building covers an entire city block. The key that unlocks the door to that building takes up very little space in your pocket. Yet that key permits you to make a complete inspection of everything in that building. Stored-up knowledge about a particular subject, profession, science, or business may be compared to this building. The key that unlocks the door to this knowledge is words. Once the door is opened, the knowledge is yours.

How to Use Key Words to Speed Your Work

On February 21, 1947, in Ripley's "Believe It or Not," under a pictorial sketch of the author of this book, was listed the following information:

EARL PREVETTE, LL.B.

COMPLETED 32 COURSES IN LAW—PASSED THE STATE BOARD OF EXAMINERS—WAS LICENSED AS AN ATTORNEY-AT-LAW AND GRADUATED WITH A COLLEGE DEGREE—ALL IN 5 MONTHS

Many people are interested in knowing how I could accomplish so much in such a short period of time. I used the key. All branches of the law, like all other branches of specialized knowledge, are built around key words. Get these key words established in your mind, and they unlock all the other doors. It seems to form a chain, and by quick review of key words, definitions, terms, phrases, and all other necessary information flash vividly before you. It is like a chain of lightning; one flash instantly blends into another flash to form the one big flash which illuminates the whole sky. One key word links to another key word, and soon the whole subject is completely illuminated and co-ordinated into a complete whole.

Speaking of key words, this is the way I made use of them to accomplish the results as told by Ripley. I reduced the whole subject of law to its simplest terms. Common law is a common sense, so I endeavored to apply common sense in making use of key words.

Law is a rule of action, to establish and maintain order in private and public affairs. A violation of this rule in private affairs is cause for civil action. A violation of this rule in public affairs is cause for criminal action. Key words, "private," "public," "civil," and "criminal."

All "private affairs" in law are based on one key word, "contract." Contract is an agreement between two or more persons based on a sufficient consideration, to do or not to do a particular thing. It is the key word to regulate all business relationships dealing with tangibles or intangibles. It deals with individuals, partnerships, corporations, personal property, real property, wills, mortgages, insurance, assurance, or any other property. A violation of the terms of a contract by either party constitutes a civil action.

A violation of the rule of action in public affairs is a crime or an act or omission forbidden by law.

Crime is expressed in "misdemeanor," "treason," "murder," "felony," and "arson." These are key words in criminal law. A knowledge of these words enables you to understand the fundamental principles of the law pertaining to crime.

In private affairs "contract" is the key word in law. In public affairs "crime" is the key word. The knowledge of law or any other subject depends on key words. To follow the simple clue of picking a key word will enable you to master any subject and to put it at your command.

As an insurance broker, I try to know the full meaning of every word connected with my business. Does it pay? Listen to this story.

I was talking to a man whom I had never seen over the telephone about insurance. He asked me the difference between insurance and assurance. This is what I told him: "Insurance is the act of insuring, whereby one party undertakes to indemnify or guarantee another against loss by a contingent event." A fire-insurance policy is based on a contingent event, one which may not occur. In fact, a fire insurance policy may be in force forever and never be a claim.

"Assurance is the act of assuring, whereby one party undertakes to indemnify or guarantee another against loss of life, which is based on a contingent event, but on an event that is certain." All life "insurance" policies are really life "assurance" policies. If kept in force long enough, they become a claim, either as an endowment when the proceeds are paid to the assured in cash, or as a death claim, when the proceeds are paid to a beneficiary. Therefore, all fire policies are "insurance" that depend on a contingency for fulfillment, and all life policies are "assurance," predicated on a certainty that *must* happen.

The man was so well pleased with this simple explanation that the commission for the business he gave me amounted to over one thousand dollars. One hundred words—one thousand dollars. Does it pay to know your words?

Every digit in mathematics has its place. Anyone out of place means a mistake. As an example: 12 plus 13 is not 21, it is 25. Substituting the 5 for the 1 corrects the mistake.

Every note in music has its place. It is the correct combination of notes that produces harmony. Any note out of place causes a discord.

As digits speak in mathematics, as notes speak in music, so words speak in dealing with people.

A lot of words thrown together may be only a noise, while if placed in the proper combination and spoken with the right pitch and tempo, they become notes and tones of power and influence.

How to Use Words

The carpenter, the mason, and the engineer must keep a close watch over the tools and instruments they use. It is these that enable them to build durable structures and do the job well. In dealing with people, you must check up on the words you put in action. The words that you use are the tools that persuade people to act. It is essential to get the real meaning and true significance into each word. "Every little movement has a meaning of its own;" so does every little word. Words must be of such nature as to carry the real meaning to others. People must understand what each word refers to, and when you get this meaning over, there is a meeting of minds. There is an understanding and an agreement. This instantly establishes confidence and makes it possible for you to present ideas and thoughts with authority. Get people to agree on things to which your words refer, and they will act.

Science estimates that people will respond to word stimuli within one- to two-tenths of a second. You can prove this by making some harsh or cutting remark to a person and see his face instantly turn red. Harsh words offend the ear and cut to the quick. In writing or speaking, by all means avoid harsh and bitter words. They sting with the tongue of an adder.

You can slap a person down with your fist, he will arise, and be your friend; but cut him with a harsh word and he is an enemy for life. Words cut deeper than swords, and their wounds are incurable.

Man could make things long before he invented words to describe them. He could make signs and talk long before he could write. His primitive nature will respond more quickly to spoken words than to the written word which represents his cultural training. Words spoken are sound signals and a means of getting the quickest reaction and, in many cases, the best response. Pay strict attention to your spoken words. As Dickens so aptly said: "A word in earnest is as good as a speech."

Disputes and sometimes heated arguments may instantly be allayed by consulting the dictionary. At our house we have one or two dictionaries always at hand. In the case of a word in dispute as to derivation, meaning, usage, or correct pronunciation, the dictionary is immediately consulted, and everyone is satisfied. The "dictionary habit" is a good one to cultivate and many useful words may be added to your vocabulary by using it.

Simple Words for Best Results

Beware of using big words and technical phrases. Verbal ghosts and hifalutin talk may sound good, but they do not mean anything to people. To direct the thoughts and actions of people successfully, you must use plain, simple words that they can understand.

The late Will Rogers once said: "I'm just a plain old cow-hand from Oklahoma, trying to get along; and as long as I remain a plain old cow-hand, I will get along and be able to eat." There is a great lesson in this for everyone, especially with respect to the use of words. As long as you present your thoughts and ideas in a sincere, plain, old-fashioned way, the results will speak for themselves.

Certain words, according to psychologists, produce an emotional reaction in most people. The word "lemon" makes your mouth water. "Roast beef" creates gastric juice and makes you feel hungry for a minute. Some words cause your hair to stand on end. Some cause your heart to beat faster. Therefore, words are a very potent influence on people, and by speaking the right word you can always get people to say "yes."

Napoleon had generals who were a foot taller than himself, yet they obeyed him. These generals did not dread Napoleon's physique. It was the words he used that made these generals move and caused thousands of people to follow him. Men can be subdued or led to victory by words.

The sale of any merchandise, service or proposition depends largely on the words used by the salesman. The salesman who uses the most colorful words, with the most feeling and meaning, is the one who usually leads the sales force.

How to Find the Right Words

Using the right word for the right occasion is no trick. It is an art anyone can develop by studying the meaning of words and their application. Speak and write in words that others may understand.

In dealing with people, study and analyze the words you use. Catalogue a few key words; around these build your conversation and write your letters. Of course, you can vary them with the occasion. Say the words aloud, pronounce them correctly, and try not to use dull words, flat words, or words with no feeling. Speak to someone about the words that you may think are doubtful, and endeavor to find out if what you are saying is being

understood the way you want it to be understood. The words
that signify meaning, and words that sparkle with meaning, are
the words you want to use. Words that simplify things, and
simplify the utility of them are the correct words to employ.
Use little words with hooks that catch the attention. Use apt
words and they will nail your message to the minds of people.

The application of words starts with an idea in your mind.
The words you use are the tools to get that idea over. A point
with an idea, presented with right words, hits the bull's-eye
You live in a practical world, you deal with practical people,
and for their sake and for your pocketbook's welfare, it will
pay you to use plain, popular, every-day words with a practical
meaning. No one can prevent you from using big words and high-
sounding phrases, but they may prevent you from being properly
understood.

Therefore, in conclusion, let me suggest that you analyze
yourself, analyze your job or position, and analyze every word
you use in your occupation, regardless of what it may be. Put
yourself in the other person's shoes. Ask yourself: Do these
words appeal to me? Would they make me act? Would they persuade and convince me? If you think they would, they will have
the same effect on the other people. Words usually react on all
of us in about the same way. If you study words, they will talk
back to you and reveal many hidden secrets that mean much to
you. Knowing the full meaning of words teaches you to spell and
pronounce them correctly, and they become magnets to attract
others to you. A robot or a parrot never varies. They put no
sense in words. You can put both sense and feeling in them.
Words, like music, when harmonized, convey not only meaning
but feeling. Hard hearts wilt in the flame of kind words, and
when spoken softly and gently, kind words render a good and
lasting influence. The good, the joy they will bring, no one can

tell. A command of words qualifies you to present thoughts and ideas clearly, forcefully, and convincingly. They are the tools you use every day to promote business, create plans and establish social relations. The correct words qualify you to do this with efficiency, grace, ease and charm. Use "The Key to a Fortune" and help yourself.

Chapter 12

WHAT CONSTITUTES A FORTUNE?

Whenever I see, or use, the word "fortune," I wonder how many people put the right construction on it and how many construe it in terms of their own self-interest.

"Fortunate," according to the dictionary, "implies that success is obtained by the operation of favorable circumstances more than by direct effort." That, however, is not the theme of the previous chapter.

The Key to a fortune is not luck but labor. There are cases, of course, where circumstances beyond our control are auspicious and we are, without any exertion on our part, the beneficiaries of chance. But chance is fickle. The only sure road to fortune is Work.

But just what is fortune?

Obviously, its meaning varies according to the dreams, or the avarice, of those who court it. One man's idea of a fortune is a million dollars. Another man thinks in terms of enough for comfort and security. The second man is more sensible than the first; because the man who is content with a conservative approach is much more likely to achieve his aims than a man who is obsessed with delusions of grandeur.

It is perfectly rational for a man to think in terms of a million dollars or even ten million, provided such a sum is within reasonable range of his capabilities. The fortune we seek should bear some relation to what we have to offer in ability and vision. Unless he is competent to organize a trucking corporation, a truck-driver who talks glibly of making a million is pursuing, not fortune but foolishness. He is thinking of a windfall that shall fall into his lap independent of the vacuum in his head. And there are thousands like him.

Most of us think of fortune in terms of excess; few of us associate it with moderation. Now that, in my opinion, is a totally distorted conception of what fortune is or should be. Fortune, as I see it, is, actually, such a substantial improvement in our financial condition, that it relieves us of many petty anxieties and frees us for a larger and more abundant life. What is fortune to one man may be peanuts to another, and vice versa. And this, it seems to me is plain: A man with an acre of land and house on it without a mortgage is better off than man who covets the earth and loses his shirt in the pursuit of avarice.

Small fortunes are more permanent than large ones, for they are easier to protect. They are also easier to organize. Every street corner in the United States holds forth the promise of fortune to somebody. You don't have to be a director in forty corporations to be a financial success. You simply have to make the most of the opportunities around you. And even what seems a small prospect may lead to great things. Some of the most fabulous fortunes in America have been founded on the corner newsstand. Department stores, banks, and great industries have proceeded from the humble operation of peddling papers. Obviously, more than papers were involved. The newsvendor was thinking. He realized that fortune is not something that is handed to you like a winning ticket in the Irish Sweepstakes, but something that you go out and seize boldly yourself.

Of course, the dream of a great and meteoric fortune still persists in the minds of most Americans, induced by the sudden and fabulous wealth that accrues to so many people in so many walks of life in this country. To-day, legislation and taxes make the transition from rags to riches, so to speak, a little more difficult, but the opportunities for affluence in America are still the wonder of the world. And the answer is not far to seek. Aside from the enormous natural resources of the North American continent, and, of course, encouraged by those resources, this country is the happy hunting ground of the man with ideas. In the vernacular, that is the big pay-off in every American activity. America is the most generous country on earth to the man who can devise new formulas for improving old methods of doing things. And it is particularly the friend of the man who can come up with an idea that entails the beginning of a new industry. The idea doesn't have to be basic; it may even be frivolous: a candy, a chewing-gum, or a more effective perfume: but so long as it is a successful means of tapping the public pocket, it is assured of a wide and profitable reception in the American economy.

In every industry, every profession, ideas are what America is looking for. Ideas have made America what she is, and one good idea will make you what you want to be. So, if your heart is set on riches, think up something that is out of the ordinary and calculated to give a fillip to public interest, as well as a lift to your personal aspiration for recognition and reward.

I want here merely to observe that there are two kinds of fortune. One is the reward of work. The other is the reward of originality and ingenuity. The second is more profitable than the first, but the first has some advantage over the second: it is accessible to all. Everybody can accumulate a competence through industry and thrift, and a competence in these times is a fortune, modestly considered. If, on the other hand, your financial goal is higher than the average, your contribution must also be higher than the average. Do something that has not yet been done and the world is yours. But always remember that honest industry and plain thrift are a fortune in themselves.

Chapter 13

HOW TO GENERATE
ENTHUSIASM

It was Christmas Eve, and Old Bob was busy as a bee delivering packages. He was singing with joy. At midnight someone asked Old Bob why he was so happy and working so late. His answer was, "I don't want to disappoint any children on Christmas morning." Old Bob had enthusiasm.

What is enthusiasm? Enthusiasm comes from two Greek words —"En," which means "in," and "theos," which means "God" —"in God." To be inspired or possessed by God is enthusiasm. It is a strong feeling on behalf of a cause or a situation. An ardent and imaginative zeal or interest that actually flames with action. Victor Hugo said: "Enthusiasm is the fever of reason." Emerson said: "Enthusiasm is the height of man, the passing from the human to the Divine." Lamartine said: "Enthusiasm is the best thing derived from history." Pasteur said: "Enthusiasm is the contemplation of the inner God." Epre said: "Enthusiasm is the invisible, inward, intensity of being."

Enthusiasm is the feeling within that inspires and prompts one to act without thought of reward. It is that inspiring, vitalizing, propelling power that takes possession of an individual and causes him to lose himself in what he is doing. It is the most powerful form of energy that one can generate. The influence of enthusiasm on the human mind and body is as demonstrable as that of breathing. Its results can be measured in terms of increased physical vitality, greater intellectual buoyancy, moral stamina, and a deeper understanding of the realities underlying all human action. Enthusiasm lights up the whole human consciousness, floods every cell with energy, puts sparkle in the eye, and scintillates in the entire personality.

Enthusiasm is so important to stimulate the function of ability that it is only proper to uncover and to reveal certain principles essential to generate it. If it were possible to take a man apart, to generate enthusiasm would be quite a simple process. However, man is an individual made up of physiological qualities, psychological attributes, and spiritual aspirations. Each of these is a contributing factor in generating enthusiasm. As an individual, man must live with all of his component parts. He has interests, instincts, appetites, urges, and impulses that sponsor his desires. He has courage, faith, and determination that sponsor his ambition. He has thought, intellect, and reason that sponsor his knowledge. These are all separate attributes that live under one roof and are confined to one house, the human body. The wisdom exercised in the harmonious use of all the different qualities and attributes of the individual largely determine the quality and quantity of enthusiasm. Enthusiasm is the very soul of man in action and is the product of harmonious relations existing in his physical and mental attributes.

The enthusiasm of an individual cannot be measured or proved as a mathematical proposition or as a chemical formula. The proof of enthusiasm can only be tested by its practical consequences, and each individual must prove it for himself. If it succeeds in obtaining results, then it proves itself. "By their fruits ye shall know them." Nothing I say proves any quality of enthusiasm. It is like the wind, you cannot see or prove it, but you can feel and see its effects.

Enthusiasm springs from order in the human consciousness, and this can largely be controlled and guided by the individual. To generate it, each individual must follow certain principles, and in my own experience the following ones have proved very valuable.

1. Preparation

The first principle to generate enthusiasm is preparation. The elements are loaded with forces to make electricity and are instantly available for conversion but, to convert these forces, preparation must be made. A magnetic field must be set up, and a dynamo installed to cut the lines of force. This preparation instantly converts physical power into electrical energy and this generates electricity. This same principle is necessary to generate enthusiasm. Enthusiasm is instantly available at all times but, to generate it, preparation must be made. Preparation is the act or process of making it ready for use.

Discipline is the first requisite to preparation. The physiological aspects were covered rather thoroughly in Chapter 9 on "How to Double Your Energy." By following out the suggestions outlined in that chapter, the physical side of man will be well fed and well treated, and this will produce sufficient energy for the body to function with zest and harmony.

On the Temple of Apollo at Adelphi are inscribed two Greek words of wisdom. Those words are "Meden Agan;" translated, they mean, "Nothing in Excess," which is temperance. The human body is a liquid mass and is constantly renewing and readjusting itself to its environment. When well fed and well treated, nothing can harm the body but abuse. Abuse is turning away from the right use of things. Excessive indulgence becomes a vice and deteriorates the body, impairs its full and complete performance and hinders its harmonious function. Excessive stimulants and excessive food cause toxins, which poison the blood and slow down the efficiency of the body. The body tormented with toxins and weakened with excessive indulgence cannot generate enthusiasm.

By practicing the principles as outlined in "How to Double Your Energy," there is no occasion for anything in excess. The body will not overeat nor undereat, and it certainly will have no need for stimulants of any kind. Each day practice the principles outlined in: "How to Double Your Energy" and the physical man will function harmoniously and efficiently. This produces energy and inspires action. It generates enthusiasm and puts you on the job with full steam.

In the field of action you will find other principles to help your enthusiasm.

2. Ask Questions

The second principle to generate enthusiasm is: ask questions. Begin to ask questions. Every question has a hook on it, and if you put out enough hooks, you will gather some valuable information and ideas. To associate and assimilate this knowledge in the light of your own experience generates enthusiasm. Ask yourself all kinds of questions concerning your ability, your ideas, and your progress. Question what you see, hear, read, and study. The only way to find out the facts is to ask questions. Facts turn into knowledge. Knowledge turns into faith and power. This generates enthusiasm.

Enthusiasm is catching. Questions not only generate enthusiasm in you, but they also generate enthusiasm in others. I can best illustrate this point by relating a personal experience. During my summer vacation, while attending college, the proprietor of a small-town hotel asked me to manage it in his absence. The first act of my management was to ask questions. I questioned every employee from the bell boy to the housekeeper. I asked each one questions on how to improve the services of the hotel. I installed a question and answer box and gave out prizes. I treated every employee as a unit of intelligence, and the service was improved over 100 per cent. The bus driver at the station, instead of idly standing around waiting for customers, could be heard proclaiming in a dignified tone of voice: "Make Hotel Apex your home while here, excellent rooms, hot baths, delicious food, and delightful surroundings."

Under my management, recognizing a simple principle to generate enthusiasm, we were one big family, eager and willing to help each other. Even the guests felt the glow and warmth of our enthusiasm. The business of the hotel doubled in three months.

Some years ago in line with selling life insurance by telephone, I had another experience that illustrates the value of questions to generate enthusiasm. I called a manufacturer, whom I had never seen, on the telephone. After presenting my sales plan, his reaction was: "I am not interested in life insurance, and I think you would be wasting your time to talk to me about it." At that point I had no more to say about life insurance, but I turned on the question box. I asked him how business was, and how he felt about things in general. This started the flow of enthusiasm. He was anxious to talk. In the course of his remarks, he told me that his company had recently built a new addition to the plant at a cost of $80,000. I asked him if they had a mortgage against the plant building and he told me that the company had a mortgage of $50,000. By this time my own enthusiasm was boiling. I felt an opportunity to be of genuine service. I feelingly remarked: "Your company, Mr. Manufacturer, possibly would be interested in a plan of insurance that would liquidate and protect that mortgage all at the same time." "What do you mean?", Mr. Manufacturer said, raising his voice. "I simply mean this, Mr. Manufacturer, that if you can pass a physical examination I will work out such a plan for you." He was examined and I placed a $50,000 ten-year endowment policy on his life, which guaranteed to pay off the mortgage at the end of ten years, or at any time before if Mr. Manufacturer should pass away, thus protecting and liquidating the mortgage at the same time.

It all started from a question.

I think it was the late Charles Schwab who said: "I consider my ability to arouse enthusiasm among the men the greatest asset I possess, and the way to develop the best in a man is to ask him questions about his work. This encourages him and demonstrates my appreciation."

Ask enough questions and you will find the answer. Asking questions starts an endless chain of ideas, each one suggesting several others. Most inventions and improvements are the result of questions. Someone wanted to know the answer.

Charles F. Kettering, vice-president of General Motors, by asking questions, generated enthusiasm to produce a paint that would dry on an automobile in one day instead of seventeen days, thus increasing production from two thousand to fifteen thousand cars per day.

I have always questioned my ability, my progress, my process of reasoning and it has been one of the greatest forces to generate enthusiasm for improvement. It is a practical means of self-analysis, taking things apart without disturbing their present status, and affords an excellent means to perfect those things.

As your knowledge increases, your vision broadens, your imagination quickens, and these generate enthusiasm.

In asking questions always try to be sincere. Ask questions straight from the shoulder. Subterfuge and camouflage are only tricks to bribe a man into saying yes, and they do not pay. People are not dumb. They are open-minded and considerate. Treat them as a unit of intelligence. Sincere questions stir up ideas, arouse response, stimulate interest, create a desire, and give you the inside track on how to do things. They generate enthusiasm.

3. The Right Attitude

The third principle to generate enthusiasm is: Get the right attitude. Attitude is to study with a purpose. It is getting the right slant on the thing you are doing, or the thing you want to do. I was educated as a lawyer but I decided to engage in the field of selling. This changed my attitude, but not my ability. With this change of attitude, I began to apply my ability to selling. In the field of selling I began to analyze human motives, and to uncover the cause that made people act. Selling took on a new meaning. I discovered that it was a definite science combined with a practical art. Science taught me what to do and art taught me how to do it. I soon realized that a profession was practicing something that was, while selling was creating a sale that was not. With this new, absorbing, exhilarating, inspirational idea planted into my own consciousness, I entered the field of selling with a new zest. I liked the idea of creating, developing, and expanding ideas to help others. It gave me the spirit to sell. I wanted to sell. I did sell. This attitude generates enthusiasm.

The perfection of any business, art, or craft is determined by attitude. The right attitude toward your job taps a hidden reservoir of knowledge and experience, and puts to work every available force to aid you in the accomplishment of your goal.

The attitude can be improved by reading good books. Good books are the foundation stones of civilization. Try to concentrate a few minutes each day on some good book. It will enlarge your capacity to understand. It will improve your attitude toward your present occupation. It will inspire you to love your present work. It will generate enthusiasm.

Speaking of studies to help improve your attitude, read this from Bacon's "Essay on Studies":

"Studies serve for delight, for ornament, and for ability. Their chief use for delight is in privateness and retiring; for ornament is in discourse, and for ability is in the judgment and disposition of business. Read not to contradict and confute; but to weigh and consider. Reading maketh a full man; conference a ready man; and writing an exact man. And, therefore, if a man write little, he had need have a great memory; if he confer, he had need have much cunning to seem to know that he doth not. Histories make men wise; poets make men witty; mathematics make men subtle; natural philosophy makes men deep; moral philosophy makes men grave; logic and rhetoric make men able to contend. Nay, there is no problem, no condition, no impediment of the wit but may be wrought by fit studies."

4. Pulling Together

The fourth principle to generate enthusiasm: Pull together.

Do not segregate. Do not hibernate. Do not procrastinate. Do not hesitate. But by all means *integrate*. Pull yourself together.

Hold a magnifying glass in the sun and see how quickly the rays will burn a hole in paper. Concentration of the rays is the answer.

To do any job well requires concentration of thought. Concentrate and pay strict attention to what you are doing. A complete integration of your mental attributes produces equilibrium, balance, and poise. They give you the power to perform with efficiency. The ability is synchronized into a complete orchestration, and the job is done with pleasure.

Peeling potatoes, shelling peas, picking blackberries, mowing the lawn, plowing the field, digging a ditch, making biscuit, driving an automobile, selling by telephone, running corporations, analyzing accounts, auditing books, reading books, pleading a case, preaching a sermon, presenting a plan, writing a book, or doing anything else can be done efficiently by conscious attention. Every occupation has interest. Put yourself into it. Pull together. The satisfaction of a job well done generates enthusiasm.

The other evening the cook was out. A friend came to call about dinner time. I love to cook. She loves to eat. The subject of hot biscuits was mentioned. A couple of minutes later she said: "I thought we were going to have hot biscuits?" I told her the biscuits were in the oven baking. She could not believe that I had made hot biscuits so quickly. Strict attention to the job will make biscuits or do anything else.

Occasionally I conduct a Sales Clinic here at the Bellevue-Stratford Hotel in Philadelphia. Men come to these Sales Clinics from all over the country, even as far west as California. They do not come to see me, but to share the ideas revealed through me. At the last Sales Clinic, I started to reveal ideas at 8 o'clock in the evening, and at 11:30 o'clock the Clinic adjourned. No one seemed tired and most of those present said that it seemed only a very short while. The secret of this performance was enthusiasm. It was a complete integration of ideas harmoniously expressed and received by all present. There seemed to exist a complete synchronization of ideas. It would be impossi-

ble for me to interest a group of people for three and one-half
hours unless there existed a concord of harmonious thought, engendered by enthusiasm.

Concentrate and pull your forces together. It turns work into
a hobby. Laziness, indolence, indifference, and stupidity give
way to alertness, earnestness, activity, and efficiency. Inject
yourself into the job, lose yourself in what you are doing, and
you will not be conscious of time or effort. Apparently this is
what happened to me at the last Sales Clinic. I was conscious of
neither time nor effort. I like to think of enthusiasm as the
Spirit of God taking over, blending everything into a kindred
feeling of understanding. It generates enthusiasm.

5. *Look In*

The fifth principle to generate enthusiasm: Look in.

Aristotle said: "We are the fragments of what man might
be." Man is inclined to contemplate himself through glasses
colored by doctrines, creeds, beliefs, superstitions, and illu-
sions. Some of these old shibboleths exert a mighty influence
and are inclined to hold man in subjection. Analyze these things
and take the best parts of them for your own enlightenment.
Do not be a slave to any of them. Throw all excess baggage
overboard. Break any chains that hold you. Endeavor to get a
true picture of yourself and evaluate and appraise yourself in
the light of your own intelligence. You will realize your own
completeness and your ability to perform.

Why not take a good dose of introspection now and then to
purge you mentally? Look in on yourself, and purge your consciousness of all impurities. They disrupt harmony and unity
and hinder enthusiasm. A good mental purge enlarges your
horizon, and affords you an opportunity to utilize your knowl-

edge and power. It helps you to get rid of frustration and discord, and you get the full power of your ability.

Look in every now and then. Look at yourself and your acts in the light of reason. It is there to guide and direct you. By looking in you will find the inner man, the master mind, and the source of enthusiasm. Remember that reason is the seat of judgment and gives you absolute dominion over your thoughts. Use it, and you generate enthusiasm.

6. Clear Conception

The sixth principle to generate enthusiasm is, Get a clear conception. Conception comes from the Latin words "con" and "capere," which mean "to seize" or "take." To form the proper conception, either of a material or an immaterial proposition, is to take into one's mind all its component parts. It is to grasp with full intelligence and to indulge in reflective thought which forms or devises ideas. It is to understand the meaning of words, to interpret symbols, and to create a scientific plan of action.

Edward Gibbon, a famous English historian who wrote *The Decline and Fall of the Roman Empire*, had this to say: "It was among the ruins of the Capitol that a conception gave me an idea of a work which has amused and exercised near twenty years of my life." Once a clear conception is formed, interest and amusement begin and these qualities generate enthusiasm.

A new conception of selling enabled me to reduce selling to a science. I proved by experience that selling any product or service could be obtained successfully by putting into operation the Law of Averages. I also demonstrated that the most scientific way known to put the Law of Averages in operation was by using the telephone. Selling on this principle enabled me to sell ten million dollars' worth of life insurance by telephone. This performance was a new conception of an old idea. It generates enthusiasm. Try to get a clear conception of your occupation. You will be surprised at its possibilities and opportunities. They will startle you. They will arouse you. They will enthuse you.

In a preceding chapter, "The Key to a Fortune," the purpose was to center the attention and to arouse your interest in the subject of words. To form the right conception of a word is to get its correct and complete meaning. Someone has advanced the theory of semantics. This is the study of the true conception of words and is advanced as the proper means of bringing about understanding and peace in the world. A true conception of words teaches us to understand; and, through understanding, all things are possible. It generates enthusiasm.

7. Retrospection

The seventh principle to generate enthusiasm is retrospection. Retrospection comes from two Latin words, "retro" means "back," and "specere" means "to look." It is the act, power or mood of recollecting the past. It is a review of experiences, and the examination of past events. To look back in thought often inspires us to look forward with hope. A review of past performances enables us to check up on our experiences, to uncover our discrepancies, appraise our progress, overcome our faults, mend our ways, and repair our deficiencies.

All business houses install a system of accounting which coordinates all departments of the business into a composite whole. All transactions are minutely detailed and recorded. This is a quick, visible means to determine the status of operation. Each department of the business is checked in relationship to the whole unit. Every few months an audit is made and each department is checked and compared to other departments. A balance is struck. A business house operating under this system can easily determine progress or failure. Through retrospection many businesses are saved from failure and progress is made.

The same principle of retrospection applies to an individual. Taking time off to look back into your experiences and examine your past performances enables you to analyze and improve them. You can develop and create a more scientific plan on which to operate. To evaluate your experience and visualize it in conjunction with your ability is a subtle and practical means to generate enthusiasm. The preparation of this book has been one of retrospection and each chapter was an incentive to generate enthusiasm for the next.

In I Peter (4:11) we read, "If any man minister, let him do it as of the ability which God giveth." A person's occupation is a ministry. It is rendering a service to others. It is making a contribution toward the completion of something. The perfection of a service in its detailed performance is greatly enhanced through retrospection. It conforms to the ability which God giveth and enables you to express patience, diligence, sincerity, alertness and kindness to every duty. It establishes a broader range of thought, a higher realm of insight, and perspicacity. It makes you more alert to duty, more considerate to your fellow workers, more just to those who work for you, and more loyal in your attitude to your employer. Retrospection helps to hasten the "blessings of the ability which God giveth!"

Retrospection is a scientific approach to evaluate past performances and records, and to lay a solid foundation on which to build future plans. Retrospection in action generates enthusiasm.

Enthusiasm has been defined. The Seven Principles showing

how to generate it have been enumerated. Go back and read thoroughly each principle, and get it well established in your mind. These principles are volts of power with which to generate enthusiasm. Your ability to be effective and forceful must be inflamed with enthusiasm. As a review, I will enumerate these Seven Principles:

First: The first principle to generate enthusiasm is: Preparation.

Second: The second principle to generate enthusiasm is: To Ask Questions.

Third: The third principle to generate enthusiasm is: Get the Proper Attitude.

Fourth: The fourth principle to generate enthusiasm is: Pull together.

Fifth: The fifth principle to generate enthusiasm is: Look in.

Sixth: The sixth principle to generate enthusiasm is: Get a Clear Conception.

Seventh: The seventh principle to generate enthusiasm is: Retrospection.

It is not putting in hours, but putting yourself into the hours that wins promotion, earns more money, precipitates an increase in salary, and gets you ahead. "Procrastination is the thief of time." Postponement and indecision are largely owing to lack of enthusiasm. Begin now to put the seven principles into action to generate enthusiasm. You have many incentives and urges to do things. You have an accumulation of unfilled hopes and desires, and the only way to put them into action is to generate enthusiasm and begin. In the early 19th century, John Anster wrote in a play:

> Each indecision brings its own delays,
> And days are lost lamenting o'er lost days.

Are you in earnest? Seize this very minute.
Boldness has genius, power, and magic in it.
Only engage, and then the mind grows heated.
Begin, and then the work will be completed.

The law of nature is: "Do the thing and you shall have the power." Therefore, whatever you want to do, begin it. Once you begin to generate enthusiasm, you will have all the vim, vigor, vitality, power, and force that you need to keep it up. Try it. You will get results. Your success and progress will not only be fascinating and stimulating, but it will be beyond your own comprehension.

Enthusiasm is one of your greatest assets. It is better than money, power, or influence. With enthusiasm you become the master of all these. Enthusiasm overcomes all prejudice and opposition and engulfs all obstacles. Combine enthusiasm with faith and initiative, and you can move mountains and achieve results unheard of.

To generate electricity costs money and power companies do not waste it. In fact, every precaution is used to conserve it. It is worth money, so is enthusiasm. Do not waste it. Remember "Meden Agan"—"Nothing in Excess." This applies to enthusiasm. Control, channel, and direct it with wisdom, judgment, and common sense. Jesus said: "Do not cast your pearls before swine." This is only another way of saying, do not waste your energy and enthusiasm on worthless things. Being the "life" of the party the night before may make a wet blanket out of you the next day.

Enthusiasm used with wisdom and discretion inspires confidence and makes people believe in you, work with you, and love you. It will make what you are doing, or what you are selling, be it yourself or ideas, speak with dynamic authority

and ring with the spirit of sincerity. It will turn your ability
into cash.

> The fault, dear Brutus, is not in our stars,
> But in ourselves, that we are underlings.

Chapter 14

AVOID THE LUKEWARM
APPROACH

Among the many famous stories about James McNeill Whistler, the American painter, this, I think, is one of the best. It reveals the intensity of his convictions and his impatience with luke-warm praise.

When Frederick Keppel, the American print expert, first called on the artist at his Tite Street studio, Whistler led him toward his celebrated portrait of Sarasate and, laying his hand on Keppel's shoulder, said:

"Isn't it beautiful?"

"It certainly is," was the reply.

"No," said Whistler, "but isn't it beautiful?"

"It is indeed," said Keppel.

Whistler raised his voice to a scream.

"Damn it, man! Isn't it beautiful?"

Whereupon Keppel shouted:

"Damn it, it certainly is!"

And Whistler was satisfied.

He had made his point. Excellence deserves something more than a complacent approval.

Interest Is Not Enough

There are occasions that call for excitement. Applause should match the achievement. So, too, in choosing the outlet for his talents, a man should bring to his labors the enthusiasm he hopes to inspire. A lukewarm "interest" is not enough. Any fool can be "interested." But it isn't "interest"; it's passion that moves the world.

Recently I received a letter from a young man who is dissatisfied with his present occupation and thinks he'd be "interested in selling." I could only reply that I knew of no one who would consider buying the services of a man laboring under the delusion that mere "interest" is an acceptable substitute for excitement.

All over America today there are thousands of young men who think they'd be "interested" in this, "interested" in that, or "interested" in something else, but who, in the practical sense of striking a balance between what they want and what they bring, are not really thinking at all. They are merely envious of something better than they've got and think they'd like to be a salesman or a newspaperman or an advertising man, not because they feel that they are especially equipped for such tasks, but solely because almost anything else seems to offer more opportunities than what they are now doing.

How to Decide on Your Proper Vocation

A man should give long and serious thought to what he would like to do and, still more important, what he feels himself fitted to do. He should not jump to the conclusion that his present discontent can be cured by the simple process of hanging his hat somewhere else. There is no progress in giving up one predicament for another. A prisoner in Sing Sing is no better off for being transferred to Alcatraz. Neither is a business benefited by having a man who, like a child at the window of a bakeshop, covets the contents but has nothing to offer in return. What business and industry are looking for is not the man who *thinks* he can do a certain job, but the man who is burning up with the conviction that he has the talent, the initiative, the enthusiasm, and the drive to make a success of it.

In addition to those qualities, there is one other that is a sort of sublimation of them all. It is what the Frenchman had in mind when he described a successful man as one who is too dumb to see difficulties. A crack runner who believes in his heart that he can do a four-minute mile and has that goal forever in mind will come closer to doing it than a runner who thinks he'd be "interested" in trying it some time. He may be mistaken—he may never do better than four minutes and four seconds—but he is forever right in the fury of his attachment to four minutes. The race is not to the "interested," but to the "excited."

How Excitement Makes Success

The ability to get excited is a rare and valuable asset. I mean the ability to get excited within ourselves about ourselves. Millions get excited over a murder or a horse race or a ball game, often because they have nothing within themselves to get excited about. I speak here of the excitement that generates its own power and is not dependent on public spectacles for its private enthusiasms. That doesn't mean we shouldn't go to a ball game. But a man is in a poor way who cannot find any occasion for excitement within the orbit of his personal being in relation to his hopes and opportunities.

Being "interested" in something, particularly in something that concerns your future well-being, isn't enough. Interest, in the sense of self-interest, is useful only in proportion to its intensity. A man interested in selling can meet a lot of people interested in buying, but they seldom get any further than being interested. He can hardly hope to induce in others an excitement he doesn't feel himself. And in case you think (as I hope you do) that calm is an even more estimable quality than excitement, let me add that calm and the kind of excitement I am talking about are often one and the same thing. There is no calm to match the calm that is the outer manifestation of an inward evangelical enthusiasm. I have seen men so carried away by a product or an idea, so head-over-heels in love with a conviction, that they were compelled almost to silence in order to keep a check on their emotions. I am, of course, recalling unusual men, but where else shall we go for our examples?

Truly successful men are not actually silent men, but quiet men, men too busy within themselves to waste or impair their concentration by giving advance notice of their intentions. They know that a premature display of their own enthusiasm weakens their chances of success and that the fanfare that precedes a project is detrimental to its fulfillment. They keep their own counsel and thus protect themselves against influences dispersive of their aims. Yet it is a mistake to think that the outward calm of a great conviction deceives anybody. People sense the ferment and the fervor that lie behind the calm, and the more a man plays down the great news within himself, the more he stimulates curiosity for details. But whether you are talkative or secretive, voluble or silent, don't ever expect people to get excited about something in which you are merely "interested."

Failure is lukewarm.

Success is "hot."

Chapter 15

THE MOST INTERESTING THING
IN THE WORLD

Some years ago I was instrumental in sending out a questionnaire to several hundred leading people throughout the country, whose activities covered every phase of human endeavor. The questionnaire simply asked: "What do you consider the most interesting thing in the world?" The answers received were as different as they were interesting. Some said life; some said love; some said nature; some said religion; some said art; some said sculpture; some said education; some said science, and some said business. Some said one thing and some said another. All were right in a way.

Don't Underestimate Your Ability

The most interesting thing in the world is You. It is only proper and fitting to pause a moment and appraise You by giving a few estimations that may inspire you to greater achievement. Seldom do you appreciate what you are or what you are capable of doing. It must come from some outside source. You take yourself too much as a matter of fact. You have not taken time to take stock of yourself, to analyze your capacities, to realize fully your strength and power, and really to discover

119

what a wonderful creature you are, nor to uncover the latent forces and abilities you possess. You forget that:

"Ye are the salt of the earth." "Ye are the Light of the World." You forget that you are the most wonderful thing that God ever created. You fail to remember that Mind and its ideas have dominion over the earth and all things in it, making you the Master. You must be reminded that it is You who can think, who can comprehend, who can co-ordinate, who can analyze and visualize, who can imagine and dramatize, and see a completed thing from the blueprint. You merely take as a matter of course that it is You who invent, discover and build the marvelous things around you. It is You who harness the forces of nature and turn those forces into light, power, and heat, to make the world comfortable. It is You who can mix ideas with natural resources and turn them into economic values, to be enjoyed by all. It is You who have the faith, the vision, the determination, and the courage to turn your ability into cash, and to plant ideas that will not only enrich your life but also that will make America a better nation—a better place in which to live.

You lose sight of yourself through the mass of things you create. You get lost among your own things. You must come out in the open and make yourself known.

There is an old Hindu legend that at one time all men on earth were gods. Man sinned, abused his privilege, and destroyed his right to enjoy his Divine Heritage. The Brahma God, the God of all Gods, decided to remove the God-head from man. He was very much puzzled as to what to do with it. He wanted to hide it where man himself would be unable to find it. Rather than assume this great responsibility, the Brahma God decided to call a meeting of all the other Gods to help him decide where to hide man's God-head.

The God of Isaac, God of Jacob, God of Abraham, God of

Truth, God of Spirit, God of Soul, God of Love, God of Principle, God of Peace, God of Wisdom, and all the other Gods met in a great conclave to make this decision.

The Brahma God asked for suggestions. One God suggested that the God-head be removed from man and placed on the highest mountain peak. The Brahma God said: "No, do not hide it there. Man will climb the mountains and he will scan its highest peaks and find it."

Another God suggested that the God-head be buried down deep in the ground. The Brahma God said: "No, do not hide it in the ground. Man will dig in the ground searching for gold, silver, and other precious metals, and there he will find it."

Another God suggested that they sink it in the deepest part of the ocean. The Brahma God said: "No, do not hide it in the bottom of the ocean. Man will dive and search out the bottom of the seas and there he will find it."

Finally, the God of Wisdom said: "Then, let us hide the God-head down in Man himself." "Yes," the Brahma God said, "we will hide it there, because Man will never think to look for it within himself."

The Power Inside Every Man

So the God-head has been hidden in Man ever since. It is still there. Most men are constantly digging, climbing, searching, looking for it everywhere but the right place. They are trying to find it from without.

Turn within, and there you will find your God-head. The moment you find it you will come to a conscious realization of this great creative force within you. That great force, that untapped power, that dynamic something, that unconquerable soul within you is yearning for expression. It is asking for recognition. It is begging for an opportunity to lift you up and aid you to greater achievements. This great creative force within you is an imprisoned giant which when unleashed can carry you on to a success undreamed of.

"The smartest man in the world is the man inside you," said Dr. Frank Crane. "By that other man inside you—I mean that Other Man within each one of us that does most of the things we give ourselves credit for doing."

Diamonds at Your Feet?

The Boer farmer sold his farm at Kimberley, South Africa, because he could not make a living on it. That farm today is the site of the Kimberley diamond mines, one of the richest spots on the face of the globe. Dr. Russell H. Conwell tells a similar story in "Acres of Diamonds." The story is about a Pennsylvania farmer who sold his farm to join his brother who had struck oil in Canada. The new owner, in looking over the farm, found that where the cattle came to drink from a little creek, a heavy scum was washed down by the rains from the ground above. The scum was examined and found to contain oil. That farm turned into Oil City, Pennsylvania, one of the richest oil centers in the world.

You may be like one of these farmers. You may be looking for richer fields elsewhere when those riches are right within you.

The most undeveloped field in this country, the richest mine that you will ever know anything about, lies right under your hat—right above your collar. At this very moment this great mine is waiting for you to develop it. What it will yield, what it will produce, nobody knows, not even you. You will never know the unlimited resources at your command until you begin to dig into them. By searching you will discover hidden powers and latent abilities that you never thought existed. By digging *y*ou will uncover thoughts and ideas that will not only enrich your pocketbook, but also that will fill your life with a fuller and deeper appreciation. By sifting, you will see an infinite variety of opportunities. A new world with untold wealth will be revealed to you, things that you never dreamed of. You will have a fuller, richer, and more beautiful life.

Huxley once wrote to Kingsley: "The most sacred day in a man's life is when he can believe in something. Faith is reason grown courageous, all progress and all science are the result of Faith."

The Greatest Faith You Can Have

You can have faith in some superstituion. You can believe in luck. You can have confidence in some outside leadership. But the greatest faith is to believe in the great God within you.

"Know ye not that ye are the Temple of God, and that the Spirit of God dwelleth in you."

Before he passed away, someone asked the late Dr. Charles P. Steinmetz, the electrical wizard, in his opinion, "What branch of science would make the most progress in the next twenty-five years?" He shrugged his shoulders, knitted his brow, put his hand on his head, and thought for several minutes, then like a flash replied: "Spiritual Realization. When man comes to a conscious vital realization of those great spiritual forces within himself and begins to use those forces in science, in business, and in life, his progress in the future will be unparalleled."

It was drawing on this great creative force, this great invisible spirit within that turned John D. Rockefeller from a hollow-chested bookkeeper into the richest man in the world. It was this force that turned Andrew Carnegie from a ten-dollar-a-week bobbin boy to the steel king of America. It was this same force that turned a puny corporal into the world's greatest general—Napoleon Bonaparte.

How to Tap the Force Within You

This great creative and spiritual force within you is greater than faith, greater than determination, greater than vision, greater than ambition, greater than confidence. It is all these combined and more. It is the very essence and substance of what you are. It is that indestructible power within. It is that dynamic hidden something in your soul. By drawing on it, by using it, by applying it in turning your ability into cash, you will double your present income and have anything your heart desires.

Devote a certain number of hours each week to study. Take time to deliberate and meditate. Take time out to read and reflect. Reading good books increases your understanding and helps you to express what other people are thinking. In doing this you are able to influence them to do the things you want them to do.

The power and force of Hoover Dam lies in the background of the tons of water stored up in it. Every turbine wheel has the full force and power of all the water stored up in that dam.

Your power and force is the background of what you read, think, feel, and really are. Once you draw on this inexhaustible reservoir, once you begin to use only a small part of its stored-up force, your progress will be unparalleled.

This great spiritual and creative force within can transcend every adversity, overcome every difficulty, surmount every problem, unravel every situation, and solve every condition and make you a veritable dynamo of power and endurance. This force within will transfer impotence into power and action. It will turn weakness, indifference, and suffering into health and strength. It will turn mediocrity into superiority. This force will teach you how to apply the great principle which Jesus came into the world to teach men: "To have life and have it more abundantly." To have it right here now in this glorious present.

This great creative force is within you right now, right where you are, ready to work for you. Put it in action, and use your ability to help you turn it into cash.

Chapter 16

HOW TO TURN YOUR IDEAS INTO MONEY

There are three separate departments of the United States Government.

First: Legislative Department. Second: Judicial Department. Third: Executive Department.

First: The Legislative Department. The function of this department is to prepare bills for legislation. After debate and consideration, the bills proposed are either passed upon or shelved. Those passed upon become laws.

Second: The Judicial Department. The function of this department is to render judgment and to determine the validity of any law passed by the Legislative Department. Is the law in harmony with the Constitution? Does it conform? Does it meet a need? These are questions which the Judicial Department may ask concerning any law. The Judicial Department can declare any law passed by the Legislative Department null and void.

Third: The Executive Department. The function of this department is to execute and to put into action all laws that have been passed upon by the Legislative Department, and that have not been disapproved by the Judicial Department. The Executive Department makes the law a reality.

The Departments of the Mind

There are three separate Departments of the Mind which deal with ideas. The function of these Three Departments of the Mind bears a striking similarity to the three Departments of the Government.

First: The Emotion is the Legislative Department of the Mind. Emotion comes from the Latin word "emovere," which means to "move out." It is a vibratory thought moving out of the mind, which is attracted by an outside influence expressed or manifested either in another idea, suggestion, symbol, or thing. It is to be aware of something instinctively or intellectually. The Emotion is the antenna of the Mind radiating and emitting thoughts into space, and also receiving them from space. All ideas, thoughts, suggestions, or impulses that come to the Mind are received by the way of the Emotion. An idea of quality and merit is given consideration and passed upon by the Emotion, which is the Legislative Department of the Mind.

Second: The Judgment is the Judicial Department of the Mind. Judgment is the act of judging the operation of the Mind, involving comparison and discrimination by which knowledge of values and relations are mentally formulated. To analyze, to reason, to interpret, and to discern is the power of the Judgment.

After the idea has been passed upon by the Legislative Department, the Emotion, it is turned over to the Judicial Department, the Judgment. The Judgment weighs every detail of the idea to determine its quality and its usefulness and to ascertain whether it meets a need and also to establish its validity. The Judgment also acts as the supreme arbiter and can declare any idea or impulse null and void, even though it has been passed upon by the Emotion.

After the Judgment establishes the validity of an idea, it is then ready for enforcement and action.

Third: The Desire is the Executive Department of the Mind.

Desire is the ardor of feeling. A longing to see the idea in action. The Desire executes and puts the idea in operation. The Desire transforms the idea into a Reality.

It takes all three Departments of the Government to make a law a Reality, and likewise it takes all three Departments of the Mind to turn an idea into a Reality. The Emotion passes upon the idea, the Judgment establishes the validity of the idea, and the Desire executes the idea into a Reality.

How to Put Your Mind to Work

An understanding of these three Departments of the Mind will help you to make your dreams come true, qualify you to have an abundance of everything, and enable you to turn your ideas into money. A knowledge of all three Departments of the Mind is essential, but the ultimate and complete fulfillment of an idea is dependent upon Desire. Desire is a combination of feeling and action, and brings into force all the qualities, attributes, and powers of the Mind.

What is an Idea? An Idea is an image formed in the Mind. It is a mental picture of something seen, heard, or thought. The formation of a pattern by which something is developed or created.

Ideas are incessantly striking the Emotion. Some are declared null and void by the Judgment. Others are consumed in daydreaming, and passed off as fleeting notions. Others take wings and fly away. Ideas come and go, and are usually dropped with a wish. Thus the old saying goes: "If wishes were horses, then beggars would ride."

A wish is all right in its place, but seldom does it turn into money. On the other hand, some of your ideas are good, and can be turned into money. On these you want to concentrate, and convert them into money.

How a Plan Can Turn Your Ideas into Money

How can you turn your ideas into money? This is a simple and fascinating process, and one to enjoy.

It matters not whether you work with people, words, or things. It is very essential to have a vehicle in which to convey your Idea to others. The best vehicle to convey an Idea is a Plan. A Plan gives to the Idea a Body. A Plan transforms the Idea into an Ideal. An Ideal is a perfect image, and establishes a true conception of the thing you want to create, or the event you want to bring about in your experience.

Everything you observe in nature is an Idea of God, and is manifested in a Plan. This Plan gives to the Idea a Body expressed in form, size, and color. If this were not so, it would be impossible to identify and classify the different varieties and species as they appear in nature. This is a definite clue as to why all ideas to influence people or to create things must have a Plan.

This great principle is manifested all about us. Everything created by man had its origin in Mind. It is an invisible idea before it is a visible thing. It is a thought, then a product. All successful ideas for accomplishment must have a Plan. A Plan not only identifies your Idea, but it also distinguishes it and gives it the momentum to operate.

Three definite Principles are essential to create a Plan for your Idea.

First: Create a Plan for the thing you desire.

Second: Develop a Process to put the Plan in Action.

Third: Produce an act to make the Plan a Reality.

A plan for the thing you desire entails a very definite and specific idea of the thing, position, or situation you want. After a definite decision has been reached, then proceed to build a Plan around this Idea.

It is a very simple process to build a Plan, and do it scientifically. It must be planned. A mass of material thrown together will not build a house. Every brick, every plank and every nail must have its place. The same is true in building a Plan. Every word, every thought, and every sentence must have its place. A Plan is organized knowledge for portraying the reasons why the thing or position desired should become a Reality. It is the art of creating in the mind of someone else a belief in the Idea you wish that person to accept.

The most scientific way to build a Plan is to get all your material together, get all the facts, and find out everything you can about the thing you desire. Get its history, background, economic relation, and the part it plays in life. Analyze these data, catalogue them, classify them, organize them, define them, refine them, and take the best parts of them and translate them into your Plan. Include in this Plan anything that will improve business, anything that will contribute to the welfare of others, anything that will add peace of mind to people, anything that will enrich the happiness of others, or anything you can find that will help you to turn your Idea into Money.

Present this Plan in sequence, enumerate each point step by step, and try to use meaty words with a picture meaning. Speak or write your Plan in concrete terms, not in abstract phrases. Make it brief, concise, direct, definite, forceful, and by all means understandable. Season the Plan with the savor of personal interest, flavor it with the spice of enthusiasm, and sweeten it with the sugar of kindness.

Second: Develop a Process to put the Plan into Action.

By inaugurating the Plan for the thing you desire you have decided definitely what you want. The Plan to accomplish this is now established. What is the next step? To develop a Process, to put the Plan for the thing you desire into action. A Process is the act of proceeding to put the Plan in operation. This is brought about by the application of Four Definite Laws, and each one is essential to the fulfillment of the Plan. These Laws are:

1. The Law of Faith

Paul gave to the world the greatest definition of Faith: "Now faith is the substance of things hoped for, the evidence of things not seen." Faith is believing and trusting wholeheartedly in the invisible forces of God which are the substance of things hoped for; and by adhering strictly to this Faith, the substance of these things will become the evidence of those forces, and make their appearance in your experience.

Someone asked Andrew Carnegie what he considered the greatest thing in his phenomenal success. He answered: "Faith in myself, Faith in others and Faith in my business." The world always makes way for the man who knows what he is doing, and where he is going.

On the evening of December 12, 1900, a young man, thirty-eight years old, was invited to speak at a banquet held at the University Club in New York. The guests at this banquet included men prominent in industry and finance, and were headed by J. P. Morgan. The topic of the young man's speech was: "The Future of the Steel Industry." He spoke for one hour and thirty minutes. His unfaltering Faith in The Future of the Steel Industry, and the Plan for initiating it were so scientific, dynamic and forceful, that all those present were moved to action. J. P. Morgan, who was expected to leave after the first few minutes of the speech, was so entranced and so impressed that he decided to form the United States Steel Corporation.

The speaker of that evening was Charles M. Schwab. As a reward for that speech demonstrating the Law of Faith in an Idea, Charles M. Schwab was made the first president of the United States Steel Corporation, at a salary of one hundred thousand dollars per year. It pays to demonstrate Faith.

Faith is a belief in the favorable outcome of anything undertaken. Faith gives life, power, and action to your Plan. Faith inspires you with absolute confidence to demonstrate your Plan, and qualifies you to turn your ideas into money. By all means practice Faith.

2. *The Law of Repetition*

In nature the Law of Repetition is continuously and regularly repeating the same things. Every day the sun rises in the east, and sets in the west, with absolute precision. The night follows the day with immutable certainty. The four seasons are consecutively repeating themselves one after the other with inexorable accuracy. The astronomer sets his clock by this undeviating law.

The Law of Repetition has been one of the contributing factors in teaching you most of the things you know thoroughly in life. For example: When you were little, it took you quite a long time to learn how to walk. Then you finally learned by the Law of Repetition. You kept repeating the same movements every day in every way. Finally, through your own experience you acquired sufficient knowledge, poise, and confidence to qualify and perfect you in the Art of Walking. In the beginning it was a very difficult task, but once you acquired the knowledge and experience of how to walk, walking became very easy.

You learned to talk by the same law. As time went on, you went to school, and again the Law of Repetition became your teacher. Over and over, it drilled you in memorizing the A, B, C's, the multiplication table, and that first poem you recited before the class. The things the Law of Repetition has taught you are embedded into your consciousness. They are a part of you and the application of them is natural and easy.

The trick of the magician looks easy. It is easy for him. He has made it easy by the Law of Repetition.

As applied to the Process to put your Plan in Action, the Law of Repetition is the act of perfecting your Plan. You do this by practice. You learn to know it; you learn to time it. You know when to speak and when to be quiet. You sense the proper pitch and inflection to give each word. You have confidence in your Plan. You learn to feel your lines, and every thought in them becomes more inspiring and more invigorating. It becomes a part of you. You can give it in perfect sequence and in perfect co-ordination. You find it has magic in it, not only for you, but for those to whom you present it. By practicing and demonstrating your Plan, it gathers its own momentum, and throws out its own aura. Your thoughts become magnets and you can make others feel the impulse of your Plan.

Every time you go over your Plan, you learn something new. You learn to develop new inspiration, new interest, new zest, and new enthusiasm. By all means rehearse and try to perfect your Plan by applying the Law of Repetition.

3. The Law of Imagination

Imagination is the power to think in terms of images, words, or things. It is the workshop of the mind. Here the Plan is given shape, form, and made ready for action. This faculty of the Mind is able to visualize and imagine an idea in action.

To illustrate the dynamic power of the imagination to develop an idea, it will interest you to know this story. Over fifty years ago an old country doctor created a very wonderful formula. He did not know what to do with it, yet he realized its great value. He took this formula to a young drug clerk and explained its contents. This formula was only an idea to the old doctor but the drug clerk paid him five hundred dollars for the idea.

What did the young drug clerk do? He turned the idea expressed in that formula over to his imagination. He visualized its value. He discovered that the contents of that formula contained all the essential elements to supply people with a cool and refreshing drink, that would make them pause and give them a lift. The idea thrilled and urged the drug clerk to formulate a Plan, to put the idea of that formula into action. He wasted no time in creating a Plan for the distribution of a world-famous drink. That drug clerk was Asa Candler. The drink was Coca-Cola. Today the name Coca-Cola is on most billboards, and the taste of it on most tongues. That little piece of paper, with an idea mixed with the imagination of Asa Candler, turned into hundreds of millions of dollars.

A sequel to this story is that some years later when the Coca-Cola Company was well on the road to prosperity, a young man walked into Mr. Candler's office and suggested to him that he had a Plan to double the business of the Coca-Cola Company. For this Plan he wanted $25,000. The Board of Directors met and agreed to the offer. That Plan was short and to the point, and possibly contained fewer words than any other plan ever offered to double a company's business. The Plan was: "Bottle it."

Imagination is one of the most valuable faculties—by all means develop it.

4. The Law of Persistence

You can have Faith in an idea, you can perfect an idea through the Law of Repetition, you can use the power of the Imagination to visualize the idea; but with all these you must carry through. You must demonstrate Persistence.

Persistence comes from two Latin words, "per," meaning "to," and "sistere," meaning "stand." To stand or be fixed, and face all difficulties with undaunted courage. To go on resolutely with your Plan, in spite of all opposition or adversity. To persevere with dogged determination until your Plan is manifested, and your efforts are crowned with success. Persistence is an attribute of character that guarantees the fulfillment of the Plan.

It has been estimated that over twenty million people have read the book or seen the moving picture, "Gone with the Wind." Something accounts for this phenomenal popularity. What is it? Scarlett, the heroine of the story, remained all through the play the master of her fate, and never its victim. No obstacle, no tragedy, no disaster, no adversity, no catastrophe, no circumstance, and no condition daunted her unconquerable spirit. She met and conquered all of them with indomitable Persistence. A demonstration of the Law of Persistence enabled her to conquer fate, and to crown her efforts with personal triumph. This demonstration was a challenge to others to emulate her. They were eager to find out how she did it.

Each year at Wake Forest, where I went to college, Doctor Tom, the old colored janitor, was invited to address the student body and to offer his words of wisdom.

Doctor Tom's great admonition was repeated year after year. It was "Be sure you are right. and then be sure to go ahead." This is a vivid illustration of Persistence.

The Plan is right, you are right, and Persistence will not fail to make the Plan work, and turn your ideas into money.

Success of any Plan is like pressing out cider with a cider press. You squeeze and squeeze and it seems as if the cider will never come; and then one big squeeze and out it comes. Persistence is the last big squeeze that makes the Plan successful. It has no substitute and it is well to remember that a "quitter never wins, and a winner never quits."

Third: Produce an act to make the Plan a Reality.

"All the world's a stage, and all the men and women merely players."

In the first Principle we acquired the knowledge essential for the Plan. In the Second Principle we learned the Laws necessary for its fulfillment. Now comes the Third Principle, the Act of Making the Plan a reality. In the last role we become a Shakespearean player. All the forces of character and all the attributes of personality must be generated to put the Plan into action.

An idea is an image. An idea with a Plan is a perfect image. It is an ideal. An ideal is something real, whether it be visible or invisible. It is a compound idea made up of many ideas. What happens when a Plan becomes an Ideal? The idea in the Plan becomes real to you. It is a part of you. The Plan is given a big reception in the Grand Ball Room of Consciousness. Here it meets urge, spirit, motive, confidence, courage, and impulse of action. At this reception Faith embraces the Plan. Imagination praises the Plan. Repetition repeats the Plan, and Persistence guarantees the fulfillment of the Plan. To visualize a Plan is to see it as a composite whole. To idealize a Plan is to feel it in action. I-deal-ize is putting the "I" in the deal. You can feel yourself initiating the Plan with skill and performing every step with alacrity and precision. You feel its influence, not only on yourself but on all those with whom you come in contact. With this power behind an idea, the Plan becomes so potent that soon it becomes a driving force behind you.

How My Plan Turned an Idea into Money

To illustrate the theory on "How to Turn Your Ideas into Money," I want to tell you how I actually do it. Some years ago, I told a general agent of a life insurance company that I wanted to sell life insurance by telephone. He said that it was impossible. A few years later this gentleman was surprised to know that I had sold ten million dollars' worth of life insurance to strangers over the telephone. To accomplish this unparalleled record it was necessary for me to know something about ideas, and how to get these ideas over to people in order to get results. I liked the idea of life insurance. This was only an idea that struck my Emotion. The Judgment passed on the idea and declared it sound. The Desire was aroused and convinced me that the idea could be turned into money. The question was how to do it?

Selling is a good deal like farming. The farmer has to plant the seed. In doing so, he has no assurance of a crop. He does know that he must sow before he can reap. The Bible teaches him: "Whatsoever ye sow, that shall ye also reap." The Mosaic Law tells him that everything in nature increaseth after its own kind.

The farmer is like the salesman. The farmer plants seed. The salesman plants ideas. The ideas of your product, like seeds, will never grow a crop of sales unless they are planted. The salesman reaps as he sows. The more ideas he sows, the more sales he will reap.

To sell by telephone it is necessary to build ideas around your product. These ideas must convey the value of the product to the prospect. He can only react on ideas. He is the negative force; you are the positive force. Suggestions must come from you. Reactions will follow from him. The ideas of your product are the seed you plant. The telephone helps you to plant more seed in a more scientific and systematic way.

Therefore, I realized, in order to have a crop of life insurance sales, I must sow a crop of life insurance ideas. I lost no time in building a Sales Plan around the idea of life insurance. In building this Plan I studied life insurance from every angle, not a phase of the subject was overlooked. I sought every available source for knowledge and information. I read every book I could find on the subject. I compared all major companies. I analyzed all important types of policies, including Term Insurance, Ordinary Life, Limited Payment Life, Endowments, all forms of Annuities and Retirement Income Plans. I reckoned with mortality tables, compound interest tables, life expectancy tables, cash reserves, disability clauses, waiver of premium clauses, and tables for optional settlements. I studied Life Insurance for partnerships, corporations, and for tax purposes. I searched tax laws relating to estates, wills, and trusts. I got acquainted with inheritance tax laws, both State and Federal. The social, economic, and financial aspects of life insurance as an institution were carefully weighed and considered. I found the institution of life insurance was the steel girder holding together the economic structure of the nation.

After getting saturated with life insurance knowledge, I began to study the prospect. Where does he fit in? Where is his place in this great network of economic, social, and financial relations? I decided that the whole system was set up for one purpose and one purpose only, and that was to serve the needs of the prospect. A life insurance policy was a declaration of financial independence, embodying guarantees that would solve his social, economic, and financial problems, and make secure his hopes, ambitions, and needs. The prospect did not know this. I had to tell him. Therefore, I made the prospect the center of interest in the Plan. I made him the hub in the wheel. I made him the spider in the web. I draped a life insurance policy around his shoulders. I idealized the Plan to him. I made it talk. I made it visualize and reveal its benefits and what these meant to him and his family.

The idea of life insurance incorporated into a sales plan of two hundred words, put in action by Faith, became a force. It arrested attention, it incited interest, it persuaded and convinced the prospect to act. It created sales, it produced results, it turned the idea of life insurance into money. (The Sales Plan I used is quoted verbatim in Chapter V under "Law of Reason.")

Ideas are inexhaustible, they are limitless. Capture one, adopt it, create a Body for it, and make a real child out of it. The child sometimes grows to be a giant.

John D. Rockefeller captured the idea to furnish light to millions of people, by the use of oil. He gave the idea a Body. At first it was a tiny baby, but twenty-five years later it was a billion-dollar giant.

Adolph Ochs, the late publisher of the *New York Times*, captured the idea to present the news truthfully and impartially and around this idea built one of the finest publications in the world.

Henry Ford captured an idea of transportation. He gave the idea an automobile Body, painted it black, called it Model T, and turned it into a fortune of over a billion dollars.

Cyrus McCormick had an idea. Around this idea, he evolved a reaper to cut and bind the wheat all in the same operation. The International Harvester Corporation was the result.

Edison gave his idea a body—"The Phonograph. His Master's Voice." He certainly had no worries about where his next meal was coming from.

All those who have made contributions in the form of services, inventions, discoveries, and science, have given their idea either a Body or a Plan. An idea can mean nothing until it is incorporated into a Plan or built into a Body.

A dwelling house, an office building, a bed, a chair, a desk, a locomotive, an automobile, a steamboat, a Declaration of Independence, a Democracy, a Republic, and even a Peace Treaty, are all ideas someone has given a Body or a Plan. An idea to be of service must be incorporated into a means of conveyance.

The Idea of Democracy (People Rule) had been in the process of development for three thousand years before Thomas Jefferson incorporated the Idea into the Declaration of Independence. In this immortal document, Jefferson defined the Idea of Democracy in these words: "We hold these truths to be self-evident, that all men are created equal, that they are endowed by their Creator with certain inalienable Rights, that among these are Life, Liberty and the pursuit of Happiness—That to secure these rights, Governments are instituted among men, deriving their just powers from the consent of the governed."

This is the soul and essence of Democracy setting forth the purpose and object of Democracy. The Declaration of Independence gave the Idea of Democracy a Plan on which to work, and laid the foundation for a Constitution and our present American form of government.

An idea takes form as it is conceived in word, thought, thing or action, according to your belief in it. Believe in your idea, concentrate on it, give it a Plan or a Body. The minute you concentrate on your Idea, new thoughts, new ideas, new measures, new ways, and new methods are opened up to help make it a reality. Drop a pebble into a pool of water. The pebble starts a series of ripples that expand until they encompass the whole pool. This is what happens when you give your idea a Plan. It seems that you tap that great creative force within. It turns that dynamic hidden something from within into a thousand friends all eager and willing to help you. It makes others feel about your idea the way you feel. It gives you all the power necessary to put your idea into action. You can persuade and convince. It makes the idea a vital, living force, the most subtle and irresistible force in the world. The idea strengthens your character and gives form, color, essence, and substance to what you desire. You can outstrip every unfavorable situation, solve all problems, and master every condition that stands in the way between you and the accomplishment of your idea. You can have anything you want—anything your heart desires. You can turn your Ideas into Money, provided you don't put money first!

Don't Put Money Ahead of the Idea

The commonest mistake of people who want to make a million dollars is that they exalt the million above the means by which they hope to acquire it.

Now, outside of an inheritance, about the only sure way to make money is to earn it, whether by the sweat of your brow or the exertions of your imagination. Obviously, the imagination yields the biggest returns, for the imagination is the source of ideas. Labor and thrift produce a competence, but fortune, in the sense of wealth, is the reward of the man who can think of something that hasn't been thought of before.

The saga of success is a saga of dreams. The vast fortunes of America have been built by men who got hold of an idea and pursued it to the end of its possibilities. They had, of course, a million dollars, or a hundred millions, in the back of their minds, but once they were convinced and assured that they were on the right track, they followed the track and let the millions take care of themselves. They knew that if the idea was right, the results would be satisfactory. They didn't worry about the reward, but set in motion the machinery to achieve it.

All over America people are fretting over their inability to make a million dollars. They are not fretting over their inability to produce an idea worth a million: they are fretting over their inability to make a million without working for it. They are looking for magic and finding only that there is no magic that can take the place of ideas. Although they covet the prize, they have nothing but a longing for money to bring to the contest. They think of money solely in terms of dollars and fail to see that what they contribute is the measure of what they receive. Get an idea and the rest will follow.

Chapter 17

HOW TO IMPROVE YOUR SPEECH, VOICE, AND MANNER

His father shook his head. He wondered what would ever become of his son who was not only frail and delicate, but who also stuttered so badly that you could scarcely understand a word he said. That lad was Demosthenes. He became one of the most renowned men of Athens, and the greatest orator of the ancient world. How did he do it? He put into action the principles of speech and voice culture, and set aside a few minutes each day to practice them. "Practice makes perfect." It worked two thousand years ago; it works today.

Everyone cannot become a Demosthenes, but anyone can improve his art of speaking. This may be accomplished through interest, conscious attention, patience, application, and a few minutes' practice each day. A large percentage of our time is consumed in talking and possibly less time and thought are devoted to the improvement of speech than almost any other activity in which one participates.

Speech has been defined as the faculty of uttering sounds, or words. It is the faculty of expressing thoughts by words. It is the power to speak. Good speech is merely trying to speak correctly so as to be understood. Speech is the quickest and most efficient means of getting your ideas over to others. It is the

143

swiftest method to communicate an idea. By taking a little pains and exercising a little care, you can do this more effectively. By checking up on the little things, your speech will improve.

One of the greatest lessons in speech improvement may be gained from the simplicity of Lincoln. When questioned, Lincoln gave this account of how he gained his ability to put "things" so that they could be readily understood.

"I remember how, when a mere child, I used to get irritated when anybody talked to me in a way I could not understand. I don't think I ever got angry at anything else in my life. But that always disturbed my temper and has ever since. I can remember going to my little bedroom after hearing the neighbors talk during an evening with my father, and spending no small part of the night walking up and down, and trying to make out what was the exact meaning of some of their, to me, 'dark sayings.' I was not satisfied until I repeated these sayings over and over, and had put them in language plain enough, as I thought, for anybody to comprehend. This was a kind of passion with me, and it has stuck by me, for I am never easy now, when I am handling a thought, till I have bounded it north, and bounded it south, and bounded it east, and bounded it west."

To be understood it is necessary to speak plainly.

What Your Speech Does for You

There are three definite reasons why one should endeavor to speak correctly. Namely:

(1) People never judge you by what you don't say. They judge you by what you say, and if you can do this well, it will influence people to have confidence in you. Therefore, form the habit of pronouncing each word correctly and speaking with care and dignity.

(2) Speech is your only means of making yourself under, stood. If you do not pronounce your words correctly and speak with the proper care, your listener may get the wrong meaning out of what you say.

(3) The correct pronunciation of each word, enunciating each syllable, will not only improve your speech, but will also make it easier for you to spell correctly.

Speech, Voice, and Manner are all fundamental parts of our living. The use one makes of these reflects how he lives. The study of Speech, Voice, and Manner develops social poise and a more desirable and pleasant personality.

The three personal attributes of character enumerated are all dependent to a large degree upon each other. The improvement and development of one means the improvement and development of all.

How to Develop Your Voice

To understand Voice Production, it is essential to know the function of each organ by which it is produced. The organs to produce speech are (1) the lungs and diaphragm, which are the powers that move the breath, the substance of which the voice is made; (2) the larynx with the vocal cords, which are voice-producing powers, and (3) the mouth, which includes the tongue, palate, lips, and resonance chambers, which are the organs that amplify the voice and transform it into speech.

Deep breathing is very essential to speech. The quality and firmness of the voice to produce pitch, tone, and inflection can be regulated and controlled by conscious, deep breathing. Stand up, inhale a deep breath of air. This presses the diaphragm down. Now slowly and gently draw the abdomen in. The diaphragm is now contracting. This forces air up through the larynx. The air passing through the larynx creates vibrations. The speed with which the air passes through the larynx vocal cords determines the sound of the voice. This sound passes into the mouth where speech is formed. Conscious deep breathing helps to control the rhythm of the breath and makes it possible to give long thought phrases in one breath. It is the secret of a good firm voice. Practice it.

It matters not what your speech may be; you can improve it by using your voice a few minutes each day. Read a few pages aloud each day. Get a list of the states and their capitals—only ninety-six names. Pronounce the name of each state and capital aloud, and enunciate each syllable clearly and distinctly. Do this exercise three times each week. It only takes about three to four minutes.

To improve the sound, volume, and resonance of the voice say the multiplication table aloud. It only takes about four minutes. Do this three times each week.

All words are formed from letters. The sound letters are the vowels. In English the written vowels are *a, e, i, o, u* and sometimes *w* and *y*. All the others are consonants. Practice aloud the alphabet, giving each letter the full use of the lungs and diaphragm, and note the different formation of the mouth as you say each letter aloud. You will notice that all the vowels seem to come out of the windpipe. To say the alphabet takes less than one minute. Do this exercise six times each week.

Stand before the mirror and see if you open your mouth wide enough when you speak. By observing yourself talking aloud, you will learn not to drag over your words. To drag out a word is much easier on the speaker, but sometimes it works a hardship on the listener. He cannot understand what is being said.

Endeavor at all times to pronounce each word clearly, enunciate each syllable plainly, and articulate each letter fully. Use the diaphragm, not the throat. Be particularly careful of pitch, inflection, tone, and volume. Form the habit of speaking distinctly, clearly, and pleasantly. Make it easy for people to understand what you are talking about. The ability to express your ideas is one good way to turn them into cash. Clarity of speech is very important. Cultivate the habit of perfecting it.

Another suggestion that may prove profitable to cultivate is the habit of not hurrying. You have plenty of time. It is most essential to clear, distinct diction to speak unhurriedly. Speak slowly and deliberately. Know what you are going to say. By knowing your lines thoroughly and by speaking them in a relaxed mood, you discover that what you say is more persuasive, more effective, and more convincing. When you speak calmly and distinctly, it is not necessary to repeat, and this saves the other person's time and possibly your embarrassment.

When talking at an ordinary rate, a person averages about three hundred and fifty words in three minutes. Therefore, take your time and speak in a decided way and with a forceful manner. Speaking clearly and distinctly prevents you from speaking too quickly. Your voice is carried most clearly when you speak directly to the person whom you are addressing. If you change this direction or widen this distance, the sound that ought to reach the listener will stray away elsewhere instead of going into the ear of the listener. When you speak clearly, distinctly, and directly to your listener, no shouting or loud talk is necessary.

Another suggestion to follow is to train yourself to speak in a conversational tone. Breathe regularly and observe proper pauses at intervals. Don't try to carry on a complete conversation in one breath.

Exercises to follow:

(1) Read aloud a few pages every day. At least three minutes.

(2) Say the states and capitals aloud at least three times each week. This takes about three minutes.

(3) Go over the multiplication table aloud at least three times each week. This takes about four minutes.

(4) Say the alphabet aloud every day. This takes about one minute.

(5) Stand before the mirror and speak words aloud for at least two minutes three times each week.

To follow through on these exercises will take only fifty-five minutes each week, less than eight minutes per day. Practice these exercises one month and you will notice a decided improvement. People will pay attention to what you say.

These exercises will also help you.

(1) Practice controlled breathing while reading aloud.

(2) Open your mouth and let your jaw relax when you speak.

(3) Articulate sounds, vowels, and consonants clearly and distinctly with your tongue, teeth, and palate.

(4) Pronounce every syllable in every word.

(5) Refrain from running your words together. You finish each word by articulating clearly the final letter.

(6) Keep all vowels, sounds, open, full, and rounded.

How to Improve Your Manner of Speech

Manner is the way you appear to others. It is that intangible quality of character that makes you interesting to other people. It is the way you conduct your relationship with others. It is an inward feeling of being happy. You know what pleases you when someone talks to you. It is nice little things such as courtesy, appreciation, kindness, and thoughtfulness. It is those things that please and put others in a receptive mood to listen to what you have to say. Those things will help you to turn your ability into cash.

Another great asset to enrich and purify you manner of speech is to learn to smile while you talk. Your speech intercepted with a real smile tells your listener a lot. It tells him that you like him, that you want to please, that you want to co-operate, and that you are willing to serve and do your best at all times. People can feel your smile, and it encourages them to believe in you. A smile in your voice unlocks the door and lets you in. It creates friendships and opens wide the doors of business and social relationships Everyone responds to a friendly smile, so practice it in your speech.

Being absolutely natural in your manner of speech distin-guishes more than all other virtues. People are human and like to be treated accordingly. People are like bees; if you treat them right they will fill your comb full of honey. If you do not treat them right, they will sting you.

One man said: "He observes others, and their acts and de-meanors teach him what to do, and what not to do."

Don't get the idea that you are too old to improve your Speech, Voice, and Manner. Anything you possess in personal charac-teristics can always be improved. Take an objective view. Study your attitude and behavior. Experiment, observe, and then elimi-nate all those little affected habits that keep people away from you. Cultivate those habits that build and cement friendships.

It requires energy to put into practice the principles outlined in this chapter. Read "How to Double Your Energy" and you will realize how closely allied Speech, Voice, and Manner are with energy. That chapter will also help you to relax, and re-laxation means freedom and ease while speaking.

Walls and barriers of resistance in dealing with others are

built by tense thoughts and rigid feelings. Relax and get rid of these. At all times cultivate the habit of speaking only when in a state of relaxation. It makes what you say click, and establishes understanding so that a spirit of confidence prevails. You speak with freedom and sincerity and what you say impresses. It rings with authority.

It takes two to make a conversation. Try to cultivate the habit of becoming a good listener. Encourage the listener to talk about himself and try to make him feel important. Do it sincerely. Pay strict attention to what he says. Try not to interrupt him in the middle of a sentence. When he wants to talk, give him the right of way. Give him full sway. He may give you a clue to some very valuable situation that might turn into cash. By listening to what he says, you compliment him. You please him. Praise his point of view and be hearty in your approbation. On the other hand, if he says something you do not like, don't tell him. Agree with him. His opinion may only be temporary, but respect it. Try to be considerate of his feelings. A kind word gently spoken is a quick means of relieving strain and tension. "A soft answer turneth away wrath." Answer all his questions. Don't ignore them. He likes explanations, and not exclamations. By all means avoid an argument, and if you find you are wrong, admit it quickly, and gracefully. This reveals to him that you are a good fellow. Harmonize but by no means antagonize.

You may apply for a position, you may seek a better job, you may offer a suggestion to improve business, you may ask for a raise in salary, you may endeavor to sell a product or a service, but regardless of the purpose and object you want to influence the listener. You want him to do your bidding, you want him to do the thing you are seeking. Then approach him with a spirit of humbleness and kindness. Feel grateful for the opportunity you have to serve him. Make him feel that any idea you are giving him is his own.

The power in a large dam of water is made available only when channeled in the right direction by the proper equipment. Speech, Voice, and Manner are the equipment to express your ability and to turn it into cash.

Words, like music, when harmonized, convey not only meaning but feeling. Spoken softly and gently, they render a good influence and a lasting impression. The good, the joy they will bring, no one can tell.

Courtesy, graciousness, appreciation, and consideration are very valuable assets in dealing with people. Use them, and remember that your Speech, your Voice and your Manner are You. They are the vital qualities of your personality. They are You in action. You can make them mechanical with no personal interest and with little effect. On the other hand, you can make them human, brimful of personal interests, and charm. You can express thoughts and ideas that will persuade and motivate. Dramatize your Speech, Voice, and Manner with imagination, enthusiasm, and color.

But above all, be natural.

Don't become too stylized in your delivery, too prissy in your diction, too affected in your manner. These faults militate against a good speech and also against a favorable reception by your audience. Don't carry your desire for improvement to the point where the improved product loses its resemblance to the original. People will detect the deception and, unconsciously, hold the affectation against you. Whatever steps you take to mend your speech, your voice, your manner, let the changes supplement and not supplant your natural aptitudes. Be yourself.

Chapter 18

HOW TO MAKE USE OF THE PRESENT

In the world today there are two definite trends of thought. One trend is based on orthodox tradition, which holds fast to everything of the past. The other trend is militant liberalism, which seeks to circumvent the traditions of the past to establish a new regime.

Between orthodox traditions and militant liberalism there is a happy hunting ground. This happy hunting ground is the world in which we live. It is a practical world made up of all kinds of people, just like you and me. No one knows where we came from, and no one knows where we are going when we leave here. There is one thing certain, we are here and it is ours to make full use of now.

It is your mission while here to make use of the common sense and reason that God has given you. You have the ability to analyze and fathom out all the events, precepts, and traditions of the past. It is your privilege to take from these any knowledge or wisdom that will help you to interpret and to understand the present.

152

A Psalm to Live By

In an article called *The Seven Great Events of Democracy*, I traced back the growth and development of democracy over thirty-three hundred years. One of the events I selected happened in the eleventh century before Christ. This is a traditional event, and for the past three thousand years the knowledge and wisdom expressed in that event have been a contributing factor in man's quest for understanding. It has been a beacon light to guide and direct man in each succeeding generation in the path of righteousness. All through the years it has given man faith, hope, complacency, courage, and determination. Through its power and influence, man has been able to conquer dread, doubt, and uncertainty. Through its inspiration man has been able to plow through the quicksands of discouragement, overcome the quagmires of defeat, and forge ahead to place himself on the solid rock of progress and good fortune.

This event is the Twenty-third Psalm. These six verses express in one hundred and eighteen words one of the most invigorating and inspiring messages ever written. It is a positive affirmation expressing absolute assurance in God as the All-Knowing, All-Powerful, All-Present, and All-Providing Shepherd to supply all of our physical needs, and to give us health, happiness, and peace of mind to enjoy all the resources of life, including the physical, the mental, and the spiritual. I have made the precepts expressed in this Psalm a part of my life. They have been a source of strength and endurance. I believe and feel them. I can heartily recommend the Twenty-third Psalm as a formula to help you make a wise use of the present.

Verse by verse this is what the Psalm means to me:

1. The Lord is my Shepherd; I shall not want.

This is a positive affirmation of Faith in God as the Supreme

Being, the Supreme Intelligence, the Supreme Ruler, and also the All-Seeing, All-Knowing, All-Loving, All-Present, All Providing, and All-Embracing Power and Spirit to guide and to direct me in all my activities. As the Shepherd guides, directs, and cares for his sheep with loving kindness, so I rely on the love, the intelligence, wisdom, grace, and power of God to guide, direct, and care for me. If I live, move, and have my being in God, then it is only common sense on my part to recognize His Intelligence, to realize His Presence, and to demonstrate His Power in my activities. A feeling of this relationship establishes unity and harmony in all my contacts and provides me with a complete abundance of all the things I need both physical and spiritual. Thus, I shall not want, because God supplies all my needs.

When I walk out in the country on a cold, clear night, and observe the skies teeming with sparkling stars, a glimpse of the universe with its infinite magnitude passes before me. I feel if God can take care of all these worlds upon worlds without end, surely he can take care of little Earl. So far he has not failed. Glory to His greatness.

2. He maketh me to lie down in green pastures; he leadeth me beside the still waters.

This is a positive statement of fact. It expresses growth, division, expansion, unlimited quantities, and inexhaustible supplies. Green indicates continued growth, and this means that God will continue to replenish the earth to take care of everything that He Creates. The only thing that wants is man and these wants are largely due to his own lack of understanding.

Pastures suggest wide-open fields with freedom to act. As an individual, I can roam and enjoy these green pastures and partake of their bounty. If I do these things with the right spirit, hundreds of people will aid me. To feel that I am in the midst of inexhaustible supplies gives me a sense of security.

"He leadeth me beside the still waters."

This statement does not say tomorrow, but it says now. To be conscious of green pastures, and a world overflowing with everything I need, destroys worry, anxiety, and dread. This feeling of security brings me in contact with the still waters, which engenders harmony, unity, and peace of mind.

3. He restoreth my soul; he leadeth me in the paths of righteousness for his name's sake.

A watch has the same works, either running or stopped. It needs winding every now and then. A man is like a watch, he needs winding. The only way to wind a man is to give his mind something on which to feed. His spirit must be restored.

In my own experience, when confusion, conflict, and discord usurp my reserve and I feel depleted, I turn to this Psalm I am now discussing and endeavor to feel its full content pouring into my consciousness. Then, like a flash, the radiant light of the All-Present Shepherd renews, revitalizes, and restores my whole being with life and power, and with a full assurance that all is well. Again, I am ready to begin anew. I stand revealed to my true self. Thus, I can sing with joy: "He restoreth my soul."

"He leadeth me in the paths of righteousness for his name's sake."

Of all the words in the English language, the one that helps me most in the paths of righteousness is wisdom. Wisdom instructs me to make the wise use of everything. In life, I deal with three principal things. They are people, words, and things. Wisdom teaches me to love and respect people. It instructs me to use the kind of words that inspire people to act. It directs me to make the proper utilization of things that build and conserve. Everything responds to good treatment. By using wisdom I find myself in the paths of right-use-ness for the sake of His name. In the Thirty-seventh Psalm, I find these words: "I have been young and now am old; yet I have not seen the righteous for-saken, nor his seed begging for bread."

4. Yea, though I walk through the Valley of the Shadow of Death, I will fear no evil, for thou art with me; thy rod and thy staff they comfort me.

Whatever the condition is, it could have been worse. Troubles are only a temporary shadow. They are a ray of sun dressed in black. Penetrate the black and there is light.

Fear has four letters. Three of these letters spell "ear." There-fore, three-fourths of the word is ear. It is largely based on hear-say. It is product of superstition. It is the ignorance of God, the lack of good, and the absence of love.

What is evil? Turn the word around and it spells "live." Live means life. God is life. If I live in harmony with God, the principle of good, evil has no influence.

When I analyze evil, I find it is only a danger signal. It is a red flag to warn of an impending danger. It means "Watch your step." As an example, an engineer on a locomotive who ignores the signal of a red flag may be facing imminent danger. There-fore, when evil appears in my midst, I know it is time to stop, look, think, and rightabout-face.

"Thy rod and thy staff they comfort me."

Rod signifies authority and staff indicates the power to direct. One of the most comforting thoughts is to realize and be conscious of the fact that I am on this earth by the authority of a Supreme Being, and to know that this Supreme Being is always available to direct me. Another comforting thought is to realize that God is a perfect Cause. Man is the effect and the effect can never be unlike the Cause. No evil or harm can touch God, the Cause. Therefore, it cannot harm or touch man, the effect. Man at all times may rest assured and fortified while leaning on the sustaining power of a Perfect Cause. When the yoke is binding, and the burden is heavy, I console myself. Thy rod and thy staff they comfort me.

5. *Thou preparest a table before me in the presence of mine enemies; thou anointest my head with oil; my cup runneth over.*

Who are my enemies? Negative thinking is my worst enemy and meanest foe. Most of the enemies of man are figments of the imagination, ghosts of dreams, and phantoms of discord. As the old man said, he had many enemies, but he could never find them. Lloyd George so aptly said: "Face one-half your enemies and they will disappear, and then face the other half and they will disappear." Under the direction of the Great Shepherd, I can feast on positive thoughts in the presence of negative enemies with absolute assurance of protection and security.

Pour oil on a raging sea and it calms the water. Fill your consciousness with positive thoughts of good, and the turbulent thoughts of discord, dread, and disunity will give way to poise, tranquility, and calmness.

Ingratitude, arrogance, dissipation, impudence, greed and selfishness are human frailties, and yet underneath all these there is hidden in the human consciousness God's loving cup that runneth over with all the good things of life. This cup contains the common denominator among all men. That denominator is Love or a feeling of kindness that always manifests itself in the hour of need. As an example: Thousands of people pass the corner of a busy street, all intent on getting some place with no apparent interest in each other, and yet let one member in that group get into an accident, and a thousand friendly hands are out to offer help.

6. *Surely goodness and mercy shall follow me all the days of my life; and I will dwell in the house of the Lord forever.*

When I know that I am in good hands, what else can follow me but good? I do not worry and fret about the next world. My motto is, enjoy the one I am now in. Why should I spoil the beauty, the majesty, the glory, and goodness of the present world, by speculating on one which no one knows? Learn to enjoy this one. If there is another world for me, God is there to take care of it. So why worry?

To practice the simple faith expressed in this Psalm admits me to what I think is the house of the Lord. That house is a state of consciousness. It is a state of harmony and unity. It is All-Intelligent and the only intelligence. It is All-Powerful and the only power. It is All-Active and the only action. It is All-Present and the only presence. When I make use of these principles, life takes on a new meaning. I put off the old man and put on the new one. The only time to live is while I am living.

How to Live Today and Prepare for the Future

"What is time?" Someone asked the Sphinx. "Time is Now," replied the Sphinx. No one learns anything rightly until he learns to know that every day is the best day. No knowledge can be of greater importance to man than to realize fully and appreciate the secret of the Sphinx. "Time is in the present." Lamenting over the past and fretting about the future robs many of the opportunity of being successful and happy now.

When God created man He gave him toes. Toes are the means by which man can grip the ground. Keep your feet on the ground. Keep your activities centered in the present. The present hour alone is yours. The past is history. It is over the dam. It is gone forever. Forget it. The future has wings. It is always one step ahead of you. The present has toes. It is always where you are. The center of the past, and the center of the future, are in the present. The past and the future are only thoughts in the present. You can think only in the present. The present owns the past, and has an option on the future. The future only completes the Plans made in the present. The best way to prepare for the future is to make full use of the present. Tomorrow is only the shadow of today. Today is the tomorrow that you worried about yesterday.

An old Chinese proverb says: "It is only the great that truly appreciate that the real great always remains as a child." A valuable lesson may be gained by observing the simple way in which a child acts. A child does not mull over the past nor anticipate the future. It is so earnestly engaged in present activities that no time is wasted in speculation. Free from doubt, free from dread, and free from inhibitions with which passing years seem to burden people, a child often exhibits a clearer, more comprehensive perception than do older people.

How Present Action Gives You Peace of Mind

The ability is the power to act, and the time to act is now. It can only perform in the present. The ability cannot function freely when it is weighed down by ghosts of the past or phantoms of the future. To function efficiently it must function freely. One of the indispensable prerequisites of efficiency is peace of mind. Peace of mind is not a commodity that can be purchased. You cannot get it in bottles, in night courses, or by taking one or two tablets before each meal. It is an individual achievement, and must be attained through understanding. The best way to achieve peace of mind is to understand thoroughly what peace of mind is.

What is peace of mind? It is harmony and unity in thinking. The mind is not static. It is dynamic. It is a continuous flow of consciousness. Thoughts of all kinds are constantly passing through the mind. When harmony and unity prevail in your thoughts you have peace of mind.

How can you establish and maintain harmony and unity in thought?

How to Destroy Mental Conflicts

The best way to do this is to eliminate conflict.

The conflict that disturbs the harmony and unity in the flow of thought is precipitated by a civil war. The battle in this civil war is between the five senses and the intelligence. An understanding of this battle will help you to put an end to the civil war and win an all time victory for peace of mind.

The five senses are incessantly picking up impressions. These impressions are conveyed to the intelligence. The intelligence, through the power of reason, consolidates these impressions into thoughts. Some of these thoughts want to start a conflict, but these thoughts have no power. The judgment, which is the final arbiter of reason, can enjoy any of these thoughts. On the other hand it can also declare any of these thoughts null and void, and by exercising this power can disarm all inharmonious thoughts at their source. This action wins the battle and ends the civil war. This act on your part makes the intelligence the big boss and you the master. Applying this principle you can manage and train your five senses and instead of being a slave to them, you can have them working for you. As the master, you can establish and maintain harmony and unity in the flow of thoughts. You can sit back and enjoy peace of mind.

Another thing to realize is that intelligence is the Spirit and Power of God operating in and through you. Nothing can harm God and no thought can harm intelligence. Remember the intelligence has the power to master any thought which the five senses can pick up.

Another aid to help you to be the master of thought is to fortify yourself from within. As Marcus Aurelius says: "Man must be arched and buttressed from within, else the temple wavers to dust." The way to buttress yourself is to practice and demonstrate your power of reason and to accept as your only companion a host of good thoughts.

How to Appraise Yourself

Another aid is to appraise yourself properly. Respect and appreciation for others starts with yourself. Do not belittle yourself; maintain your dignity and endeavor to make the most of your own ability.

A rabbit does not degrade himself or go around complaining because he is not a hawk. He becomes a good rabbit and fulfills his place in life. What you have is yours and, if you make use of it, you will have more.

Accept yourself for what you are, take the good with the bad. After all, you do not encounter angels on this plane, and if you did you possibly would not recognize them. These four lines by Edward Wallis Hoch always come in handy:

> There is so much good in the worst of us,
> And so much bad in the best of us,
> That it does not behoove any of us
> To talk about the rest of us.

It will also help you to be tolerant. Life is a compromise and to accept it on these terms is to add to your own peace of mind. A man is entitled to his opinion and tolerance is to respect this opinion without believing or sharing in it. A respect for another's point of view will always enlarge your own. As Voltaire said: "I disapprove of what you say, but I will defend to the death your right to say it." Tolerance is getting rid of prejudice and hatred. It is trying to establish a true relationship between

situations on an impersonal basis. It is a good quality to practice and pays big dividends.

How to Adopt a Constructive Attitude Toward Life

Another aid to your peace of mind is to get rid of vanity. The
world was here when you came. It will be here when you are
gone. You cannot change it. You cannot reform it. In fact, you
cannot change anything but your attitude about it. Adjust yourself to the world as you find it. Enter into your occupation with
a spirit of sportsmanship. Train yourself to enjoy it, and things
will come your way.

Another aid to your peace of mind is to have a system. It
helps you to plan your work and work your plan. It teaches you
to do things that lie clearly at hand rather than anticipate or
discount the things that lie in the distant future.

Victor Hugo once said: "He who every morning plans the
transactions of the day, and follows out that plan, carries a
thread that will guide him through the labyrinth of the most
busy life. The orderly arrangement of his time is like ray of
light which darts itself through all of his occupations. But when
no plan is laid, where the disposal of time is surrendered merely
to the chance of incidents, chaos will soon reign."

The people who do things in life, who live strong, vibrant,
joyous, happy, and conquering lives, are the ones who make use
of the present. Of course, they make mistakes; they stumble;
they fall; they encounter obstacles, hardships, and heartaches.
They do not quarrel or grumble with these adversities. They use
them as stepping stones to greater achievement.

Life says: Go on. Be finished with past. Let the dead bury the
dead. It was good. It was bad. It was weak. It was strong. Even
so, it is all over. So what?

If you have done right, keep it up. If you have done wrong,

begin to do right. Reformation and determination will defeat sin and bad habits.

An everlasting Now reigns in nature. Everything conforms to the present and takes full advantage of its bounty. The sun never puts off shining, the stars never fail to come out at night. The rose blooms, once it is ready to perform the act. All animals live only in the present. Consider the lilies of the field, the birds of the air, the fish of the sea—they never lack for what they need.

The best way to make full use of the present is to turn the heat of love on all inward griefs, all secret jealousies, all silent inhibitions, all ingrown selfishness, all sour grudges, all bitter envies, all malignant hates, and all distasteful memories. Love brings a feeling of kindness, that will relax you. It will free you from all the old skeletons of the past, and will also help you to avoid any new-hatched phantoms of the future.

Exercise your sense of humor. Train yourself to laugh. Do not take things or people too seriously and by no means yourself. Welcome irritations and they lose their power. If people are uncivil, give it no thought. Do not even consider it. Laugh it off. After all, it is not man's action that troubles you, it is the thought and consideration that you give them. Resist the devil and he will make it hot for you; feel good about him and he disappears. Maintain a sense of humor. It will relax you mentally and this means peace of mind and efficiency.

The Lord's Prayer says: "Give us this day our daily bread." This is a positive statement, a positive prayer for the present. It puts into practice the principles outlined in this chapter. As Whittier wrote in his poem, *My Soul and I:*

> The Present, the Present is all thou hast,
> For thy sure possessing,
> Like the patriarch's angel, hold it fast,
> Till it gives its blessing.

The present is overflowing with milk and honey. It is brimful of new ideas, new hopes, new adventures, and new opportunities. Let nothing stand between you and these blessings. Partake of them; use and enjoy them.

"Rejoice and be exceeding glad; for great is your reward in heaven." This is one of the great admonitions taught by Jesus in "The Sermon on the Mount." Practice this precept and great will be your reward right here. It will animate you. It will free you from all restraint. It will release you from all anxiety, worry, and dread. You will be a free man in a free world. You will know the good old days are right here and now. Heaven is here—are you?

Chapter 19

HOW TO MAKE A SPEECH

In matters of money you either give interest to get dollars, or give dollars to get interest. In either case, it is give and take. The same principle applies to those who speak in public. It is mutual. To get interest from an audience, it is necessary to give the audience something for their interest.

Nearly everyone is called upon on occasions to speak a few words in public, and to give his views, thoughts and ideas concerning different subjects. We find it necessary to make a speech.

I have been speaking in public ever since I shouted: "The boy stood on the burning deck." That was over forty years ago. In that time I have made many speeches covering a variety of subjects. I have read many speeches made by others. I have listened to many speeches made from the platform and over the radio. I have concentrated on these speeches, taking particular note of their technique, quality, and style. Through my own experience and observation and by analyzing the speeches of others, I have acquired some practical knowledge on the subject. I am passing this information along to you. The principles selected have been used most effectively and persuasively by others. I believe you will find them helpful.

Making a speech is one of man's oldest arts, and one of the quickest and most potent ways to get ideas over to his listeners.

The higher types of speech demand more than mere readiness in speech, in grace, in gesture, and a fluent command of language. Back of these accomplishments must rest superior powers of thought, logical sequence in reasoning, quickness, and brilliancy of conception, control of rhetoric, and also what is known as personal magnetism, which is the ability to sway the feeling of the hearers by expressing warmly what they are thinking. Ideas must be couched in words that convey the real meaning of thought.

How to Develop Your Public Speaking Ability

The most scientific way to develop your ability to speak before an audience is to follow certain definite principles which other successful speakers have found to be effective. Try to get a book containing famous lectures or speeches. Memorize and recite the opening paragraphs, the climaxes, and endings of the great orations until they become thoroughly familiar. Many sentences, phrases, and words may be used many times when you mix and flavor them with originality. They increase your capacity to speak fluently and give the speech a certain quality that makes an impression. Demosthenes, as well as all other famous Greek, Roman, and American speakers have followed this practice. Demosthenes had a book containing fifty or more stock perorations, climaxes, beginnings, endings, anecdotes, illustrations, and form paragraphs which he used repeatedly throughout even his greatest orations. He made suitable variations to fit the occasion.

Elbert Hubbard's *Scrap Book* contains useful material that can be applied to any speech. Stevenson's *The Home Book of Quotations*, will furnish a suitable quotation that may be incorporated in any speech. In driving home a point, an apt quotation has no substitute. It makes your listeners sit up and take notice. Read *The World's Greatest Orators and Their Best Orations* by Morris. Every man has an occasion to show his stuff, and the time to get prepared is when no one is looking. It is an advantage to any one to speak distinctly, to the point, gracefully and with genuine fire. It extends your personality, enriches your character, and will help to turn your ability into cash.

There are three bodies to a speech.

1. The Introduction. A short story, a brief anecdote or a personal experience is most effective to introduce a speech on any subject. A sentence expressing an unusual analogy is also appropriate. Either the story or the experience must be short and to the point.

2. Body. The main body of a speech must set forth the full context of the subject, consolidating all details into one composite whole.

3. The Close. It is most convincing to summarize the reasons and advantages of the main body at the close. Use short sentences, make them snappy and pungent. If possible, recite a brief quotation to amplify your own thought. Never close a speech with a funny story. "A laughing audience has a short memory."

A speech is more effective and more fully appreciated when prepared. Follow a pattern. Arrange your points in logical sequence. The introduction and the close are very simple. The main body of a speech, to persuade and convince, must be planned on the following principles.

1. Organize Your Thoughts

A speech, to be effective, must be direct and to the point. In preparing a speech, take a sheet of paper, write down every thought and idea you can possibly think of pertaining to the subject. One thought suggests another. Read all the correlative material you can lay your hands on, and make a note of every thought that will add illumination to the subject. Analyze and review this material, get all the facts, and find out everything possible on the subject. Get the history, background, economic relation, and the part that the subject plays in the life of the audience. Meditate and reflect, and by the process of elimination select the thoughts that you feel are the most appropriate. Analyze these thoughts, organize them, take the best parts of them, arrange them in sequence, and translate them into the interest of your audience.

The body of a speech is knowledge organized to portray ideas and to convey thoughts. Every word, every thought, and every sentence must have its place. To follow a pattern in the scientific arrangement of your data qualifies you to know exactly what you want to say. You do not mumble, you do not ramble, and you do not stumble. You speak with a command and your audience pays strict attention to every word. To know your subject matter, and to enumerate it in logical sequence, inspires self-confidence and an air of assurance. Instead of halting and hesitating you become dynamic, bold, and courageous. Your message clicks and becomes a living force for good.

2. Incorporate Plenty of Meat in the Speech

Most speeches are like a wagon wheel, "the longer the spoke, the greater the tire." Many "Oh—hums" and many bored audiences may be eliminated by thorough preparation. Regardless of the kind of speech, or the occasion, the audience is made up of people. People have the same likes and dislikes. You like a speech full of human interest, so do others. Human interest is fundamental. What appeals to one group appeals to another. People are primarily interested in the same things. Therefore, a speech, to be effective, must incorporate what people like. Human interest always makes an appeal. Personal experiences, short anecdotes, and little stories of success engender color and flavor. Properly timed and placed, they persuade and convince more quickly than the most eloquent utterances or the most elaborate argument.

Some years ago Henry Ward Beecher, one of the greatest preachers and platform lecturers of his day, was invited to a town in West Virginia to deliver a lecture.

In those days that part of the country was widely known in lecture circles as "Death Valley." Most speakers wilted when they faced an audience of people who were rather indifferent.

It was a very sultry day in July when Beecher arrived in this town to deliver a lecture. Beecher had been warned. He knew what to expect. Beecher was a genius in arousing the interest of an audience. In the afternoon, when he was introduced, half the audience was yawning and the other half was dozing. Beecher briskly rose from his chair and, mopping his brow with his large red handkerchief, hastily strode to the front of the platform. "It is a God-damned hot day," said the preacher. Everyone in the audience was electrified, and for a moment it seemed as though a bolt of lightning had struck the building. Beecher paused. Raising a finger of solemn reproof, went on: "That's what I heard a man say here this afternoon." From that moment a thousand eyes were fixed on Beecher. Everyone in that audience was eager to hear him. He aroused their interest and his message went over with a bang.

Some years ago, I was invited to make a speech. I chose for my subject "The Three-Legged Stool," a dissertation on the relation of Capital, Labor, and the Public. Toasts to doubtful characters and the denunciation of the Constitution of the

United States opened the meeting. I had been unaware that it was a communistic meeting.

Finally my sponsor introduced me. I spoke briefly as follows: "Some people here are denouncing the Constitution of the United States. This is the law of the land and guarantees civil rights to everyone. This law makes it possible for you to meet here in peaceful assembly, and to denounce it is to denounce your own security." At that moment someone shouted, "Go to hell." I paid no attention. In explaining "The Three-Legged Stool," I pointed out that Capital represented one leg, Labor represented one leg, and the Public represented one leg. These three legs make the stool and each leg was dependent upon the other to stand, and all three legs must stand together, or else fall together. Again the voice in the audience shouted, "Go to hell." I paid no attention. In about one minute the same voice shouted, "Go to hell." I paused, smiled, and said, "Ladies and Gentlemen, in the past five minutes I have been invited three times to join the Communist Party." The audience rose to its feet and cheered me for at least two minutes. Every person in that audience was my friend.

My friend, Ralph W. Page, that brilliant newspaper columnist, tells a very interesting story that graphically illustrates how to get the interest of an audience. A distinguished group met in New York to discuss the "Form of the Future." In the four sessions, the thought and plans of the free world were explored, expounded, and clarified. Every group had its say. A plan to free the enslaved nations was openly discussed. Prominent representatives from everywhere aired their views, and explored their own brand of philosophy. Most speakers dealt in platitudes. The apparent effect was noise against the walls. Doctor B. A. Liu spoke for China. He said:

"The design of a just and durable peace and a valid world

order calls for nothing new. All we need to do is to put the good old wine in new bottles. The old wine, the valid formula, is as old as Confucius, who said over two thousand years ago:

" 'When the Golden Age prevails, the world will become as one; rulers and officials will be elected according to their wisdom and ability; mutual confidence and peace will prevail; the old folks will be able to enjoy their old age and every youth be employed according to his talents. The widows, the orphans, and the crippled will be well cared for. Every man will have his occupation and every woman her home.

" 'No man's goods will be wasted, for he will use any surplus for the benefit of others—and those who have more energy than they need will not have to confine their labor to their own benefit.

" 'There will be no cunning and no intrigue, and there will be no bandits, and the outer gate will not be closed at night.'

"This," said Doctor Liu, "is the old wine. All that is needed is to pour it into the new bottles of present conditions. The principles are all there."

Every material consideration bearing upon a new world organization had been presented by experts. "It is significant," says Page, "that this homily of an ancient prophet upon justice, altruism, kindliness, and unity received the maximum ovation and struck the one universal chord in this erudite American audience."

It only proves that when you strike the heart chord of man, you strike his interest.

For real meat and interest, read Demosthenes' famous oration, "On the Crown," Cicero's, "The Treason of Cataline," Pericles', "The Dead Who Fell for Athens."

In Act III, Scene Two, in Shakespeare's *Julius Caesar* is the artful and eloquent funeral oration over the body of the slain

Caesar. In this oration, Mark Anthony was so persuasive that he roused the fury of the populace against Brutus the slayer, and all the other conspirators who caused the death of Caesar, and forced them to flee Rome.

In Matthew, Chapter V, is the "Sermon on the Mount." In these Beatitudes, Jesus gave to the world enough interest and meat to last forever.

The speech of Paul defending Christianity before King Agrippa, in the Twenty-sixth Chapter of Acts, is one of the most gripping speeches ever delivered. Paul's plea was so convincing that King Agrippa said: "Almost thou persuadest me to be a Christian."

An "Appeal to Arms," by Patrick Henry, was the keynote appeal for American freedom. "Forbid it, Almighty God! I know not what course others may take; but as for me, give me liberty, or give me death." These two sentences fired the consciousness of every liberty-loving patriot, and roused the colonists to action.

At the conclusion of one of the greatest speeches ever delivered in the United States Senate, the members of that body crowded around Daniel Webster, their colleage, to congratulate him on the world-famed "Reply to Hayne" and his masterful ability to make an extemporaneous speech. "Ah, no," said he, "this is not an extemporaneous speech. I have worked months preparing this speech and every cubbyhole in my desk is filled to the brim with notes and clippings."

"You can do it extempore, for it is nothing but roaring." Extemporaneous means without previous study or preparation. It is endeavoring to compose and utter a speech on the spur of the moment. Extemporaneous speeches and impromptu utterances are usually nothing but roaring, full of sound and fury, signifying nothing. They make people "ho hum," stretch, yawn, and doze, and sneeringly remark, "Why bring this up?"

Everyone knows Lincoln's famous "Gettysburg Address," and this, too, is a good one to put in your "speech-making kit." "That this nation, under God, shall have a new birth of freedom, and that government of the people, by the people and for the people shall not perish from the earth." These lines welded together the Union and preserved the American form of government.

"Acres of Diamonds," by Dr. Russell H. Conwell, was the most popular lecture ever delivered in the United States. Why? Because it was overflowing with human interest, inspiring people to practice the principle of self-reliance.

Another great speech of the last sixty years was "The Cross of Gold," by William Jennings Bryan. It was a passionate plea for "Free Silver."

In 1915 at the age of 19, I was awarded the Andrew Carnegie Medal for writing and delivering a speech on International Peace. My subject was: "Is War Rational?" The opening sentence was: "War is as old as the human race, and as young as the last breath you breathe." This sentence was quoted in newspapers throughout the world. This introduction caught the ears of the judges and stimulated their interest in my speech. The Main Body of this Speech endeavored to prove that war is not rational, by the following propositions:

First: War is an intolerable burden.
Second: War is an irreparable human loss.
Third: War is an incurable folly.

It has been my pleasure to speak before many organizations during the past few years, especially during the war. To excite interest, I began to study "The Great Seal" of the United States as portrayed on the green back of a dollar bill. In the obverse side of the seal, which is on the right side of the dollar bill, and in the reverse side of the seal, which is on the left side of the dollar bill, are seventeen different symbols. Each symbol portrays a tradition directly associated with Democracy—our American form of government. These symbols are the introduction to a speech. The main body of this speech is: "The Seven Great Events of Democracy." Those events cover thirty-one centuries of history and tend to show that Democracy, our American form of government, has been in the making during that time.

It takes one hour to deliver this speech. I use no notes. You can hear a pin drop. Everyone is vitally interested, because that speech expresses thoughts and ideas close to their fireside.

3. Choose Key Words

The chief ingredient in a speech is words, and they determine the quality of the speech. Words define your ideas on a subject and convey them to your listeners. Key Words are very important in the preparation of a speech. They are the steel girders that hold together the contents of the subject matter. They are the spider in the web. They are the hub in the wheel around which revolves the entire discourse.

To win the Andrew Carnegie Medal, in competition with many men representing many universities and colleges, I realized it was necessary to create a speech of comprehensive, but simple understanding. After a process of culling and sifting, I selected three Key Words. (1) Intolerable! Intolerable what? An intolerable burden, a burden almost beyond human capacity to bear. (2) Irreparable! Irreparable what? Irreparable human loss, a loss which cannot be replaced. (3) Incurable! Incurable what? Incurable folly, a folly as old as the human race, and one that may continue. These three Key Words were the hub of my argument to prove that war is not rational, and thus answers the query of my subject, "Is War Rational?"

People like a speaker who takes them into his confidence. They like an explanation of terms. I explain everything as if I were telling a little child for the first time. It works. In the lecture on "The Seven Great Events of Democracy," I define Democracy by giving its etymological derivation. I spell out the two Greek words from which it is derived. "Demos," which means "people." "Kratos," which means "rule." Democracy therefore means "people rule." I define "event." I define "republic," another Key Word in the speech. Republic comes from two Latin words, "res," which means "thing" and "publicus," which means "public" or "open." Republic therefore means things done in the open, or for the public. Every law enacted in a Republic is instantly accessible to the public. No law can be a secret. It is public knowledge. Therefore, a Democracy is the will of the people, expressed in the open by a system called a Republican Form of Government which is a plan to enforce that will. In speaking to an audience in this fashion, they are all ears. Try it.

In the preparation of a speech, select a few Key Words. Build your speech around these words. Define the Key Words, and explain their meaning fully. Use plain everyday words. Speak in the language of the audience. Get down to earth. Talk to others as you like others to talk to you. Study each word; analyze it. Ask yourself—are these words conveying the real meaning of my thoughts? Are they expressing my ideas? When you speak before an audience, you are talking out loud to yourself. Others are listening. Therefore, if you convince yourself, you convince others.

Therefore, to create a speech, it will help you to follow these three Principles:

First: Organize your thoughts.
Second: Incorporate plenty of meat in the speech.
Third: Choose Key Words.

The meal is prepared. It is seasoned well and baked to a crisp brown. It is steaming hot. It is ready to serve. Please do not spill the beans.

The artful presentation of a speech depends upon the speaker. How to be natural and effective when speaking in public can easily be accomplished by adhering to a few rules.

(1) Breathe deeply and fully many times. Stretch and press down on the diaphragm. Repeat the Lord's Prayer and feel its presence. Thank God for the opportunity, the occasion, and the people. Ask Him to help you do your best. These acts, lasting a minute or so, establish poise and placidity.

(2) As you rise to speak, cast your eyes easily over the audience for a few seconds, smile, and look pleased. Begin to speak in a pleasant and conversational tone. Try to be perfectly natural.

(3) Spot a person at the back of the audience and regulate the pitch and tone of the voice to accommodate him. If in doubt, ask him if he can hear you. A little personal consideration makes the people in the audience feel kindly toward you.

(4) Pronounce each word clearly; enunciate each syllable deliberately; and speak in a decided manner. Clear diction adds dignity to the speech, and makes it easy for people to hear.

(5) Do not let your voice fade out at the end of a sentence. The end of a sentence is as important as the beginning. The whole sentence must be heard or its meaning is lost.

(6) A change in the program may necessitate a change in

your speech. Vary your speech with the occasion, but always go prepared. Demonstrate earnestness and remain deliberate.

(7) Say your speech; do not read it. To read a speech is like throwing a wet blanket on the flame. You may still have the flame, but not the glow. The flash of the eye, the freedom of the body, and the smile add charm to the speaker and make the speech more convincing.

(8) Don't hurry in speaking. Talk from the diaphragm. Pause at proper intervals and do not try to make a speech with one breath. Speaking hurriedly destroys the resonant sound of the voice and your words do not have the proper pitch, inflection, volume, and tone. The sound of words plays an important part in your message.

(9) Try to keep your hands at your side in a carefree way, and only use them when you are illustrating a point or laying emphasis on a particular proposition.

(10) The best style and manner in speaking is to be natural. Try to be yourself, at your best. Talk to people in your inimitable way. Say what you mean, and mean what you say.

(11) Read the chapter "How to Improve Your Speech, Voice, and Manner," many times. It gives a myriad of suggestions that are absolutely invaluable in the delivery of a speech and will qualify you to speak distinctly and clearly in public.

(12) Be brief and concise, and talk with the people. Don't yell at them.

In my own experience, I spend many hours in organizing and arranging my thoughts before I attempt to make a speech. I feel in debt to any group of people who invite me to speak before them. To discharge this debt, I endeavor to prepare something that will be of interest. I never attempt to insult the intelligence of people with an impromptu speech or to inflict an extemporaneous one. Therefore, when I find people in my audience yawning, ho-humming, and dozing, I shall be through speaking in public.

Lord Chesterfield said: "Be wiser than other people, if you can, but don't tell them so." I always give people credit for knowing as much as I do. I never try to display how smart I am. I approach my audience with a spirit of humility, as one who comes to serve. I find as long as I speak in a spirit of humbleness, my message has power and punch.

In making a speech, you want the people in the audience to listen. To convince and persuade them, you must get their undivided attention. To do this follow a pattern. Remember first: The Introduction; second: The Body; third: The Close.

In preparing the main Body, organize your thoughts, include any suggestions for the improvement of business, the increase of income, the extension of public welfare, the prolongation of life, the promotion of health, the accretion of happiness, and the achievement of success. Feed your audience plenty of meat. Make your speech sparkle with human interest, and relate stories about successful people and unusual accomplishments.

Choose Key Words that sound well. Know their meaning. Be explicit and illuminating in your definitions.

Speaking in public is only conversation elevated to its full capacity.

All doubt, dread, and anxiety in the making of a speech are instantly removed by thorough preparation and by a feeling that you are talking to a dear friend, and do not care who is listening. An audience is a group of individuals; when you talk to one, you talk to all.

In conclusion, make your speech as you would talk. Be explicit and brief. Try to inject a sense of humor. Talk with your audience, and not at them. Take it easy, and enthusiasm will permeate the audience. You will speak with charm, with effect, with persuasion, and with conviction. You can do it. Get at it.

The floor is yours.

Chapter 20

HOW TO WRITE A LETTER

If you want to know how *not* to write a letter, I can tell you where to go for the best examples.

Consult the average correspondence of any business organization and it will give you a college education in leaden thoughts and wooden expressions.

In Chapter 5 I reproduced a letter of mine about my book, *How to Sell by Telephone.* It is not, however, presented as a model for letter writing.

It is brief, blunt, and direct, which was all it could be. It would be immodest in an author to sing loud in praise of his own wares.

The one thing responsible, in my opinion, for an 80 per cent response to that letter was the title of the book itself. The telephone is one of the most common means of communication on earth and every owner of that invaluable instrument would like to turn it to a profit.

The essential difference between a letter and a telephone call is the difference between the written word and the spoken, and the first has some advantage over the second. The spoken word, addressed to the ear, is quickly forgotten. The written word is addressed to the eye and consists of visible, tangible, permanent symbols. It obviously has a better chance of survival.

There is something about a letter that is not true of other means of communication. It has the intimate, personal touch of human contact. A telephone speaks and is silent; a letter is articulate as long as it is in your possession. One is a ring that evaporates; the other is a record that remains. A telephone hangs up; a letter hangs on. They are as far apart as a memory and a memento.

Why, then, is a telephone call usually more human than a letter?

The answer is, that we are all more natural and spontaneous when we speak our thoughts than when we write them. We are relaxed and easy when we pick up a telephone; we are tense and self-conscious when we dictate or pick up a pen. The closer the written word comes to the spoken the better; though, of course, in many letters a somewhat more formal note is necessary. But one rule holds whether you get up to speak or sit down to write: *Avoid the platform manner.*

How to Get the Greatest Response from Your Letters

A letter, like a person-to-person call, is a mental meeting of two minds. Even when you are speaking for a group and the recipient also represents a group, the personal relationship between you and him remains, at least to the extent of the letter. What you say may be company policy, but how you say it reveals the power or the poverty of your ability to express yourself.

It is true, of course, that a letter, well written or otherwise, which sets forth and gets over to the reader the ideas the writer wants to convey, has achieved its purpose. But there are many occasions in a man's life when a letter calls for something more than a bare recital of fact and circumstances. There are times when the purpose of a letter is to influence, persuade, and convince. The ability to assemble a few platitudes and string a few sentences together does not adequately meet those requirements.

The first question to ask ourselves when we have a letter to write is this: What is this letter supposed to do? We should then ask ourselves: What is the best way to do it? The first question is easy to answer; the second takes a little thought and requires the command of an easy and resourceful vernacular. Even when the subject calls for vigor, the style should be as casual as possible.

Be explicit, be simple, and above all, be brief.

Short words, short sentences, short paragraphs are the shortest way to the interest of the recipient. He is encouraged when he sees how little you want him to read. On the other hand his interest is dissipated by long and ponderous stretches of prose. Long letters are sometimes necessary, of course, as in the case I am about to relate. But, allowing for exceptions, the shorter your letter, provided it is well done, the better your chance of a favorable response.

Some years ago a friend of mine in the Chicago office of a very important national magazine, wrote me that he was having great and increasing difficulty in making contacts through the medium of his letters. He wanted me to suggest an approach that would get interviews. I have no magic in such matters but I agreed to try. I therefore asked him to send me a duplicate of his last letter.

It was, excusably, a long letter, for it was not too long in relation to the ground it covered. It told a detailed story of national and regional circulation and furnished convincing evidence of what it had done and could do for advertisers. Every facet of the subject was briefly but adequately explained. Long as the letter was, it could hardly have been more concise and compressed. For a long letter it was a good letter. The thoughts were clear, the sentences were sharp, and its points were logical and effective. What, then, was wrong with it?

Well, there are two schools of thought on the subject, but I'll stick to my own, since I presently proved its worth to my friend in Chicago.

His letter concluded with an earnest request for an interview, and it has always been my opinion that the chance of an interview recedes if the prospect knows in advance all the details of what you want to see him about. If he is interested, he will send for you; if he is not interested, why should he listen to an oral repetition of a familiar story? The danger of a letter that tells everything is that it leaves no room for further discussion.

How to Open Doors with Letters

What my friend needed was interviews; for no matter how good a long, explanatory letter may be, it still lacks the advantages of personal contact. Meeting a man in person is always better than meeting him by mail. So, I suggested and wrote a series of forty letters, guaranteed not to exceed fifty words apiece, to be mailed every other day to his most stubborn prospects. The sole purpose of these letters was to get the recipient to ask the writer to come in, and the stratagem succeeded. Within six weeks my friend reported that every door, which had previously been closed, had opened.

I can put in eight words just what these fifty-word missives did: *They excited curiosity but did not satisfy it.* And that, it seems to me, is what a letter should do if a personal interview is desired. Brevity is the best way I know of to create a favorable impression and elicit a favorable reply.

There is a French proverb that says: "The easiest way to be dull is to say it all."

Let your letter leave a man wondering what it's all about. But wait till you see him before you tell him all about it.

Chapter 21

HOW TO ATTRACT AND GET WHAT YOU WANT

Some time ago I had a dream. In this dream I awoke to find myself all alone in the World. There was no distraction, no disturbance, no confusion, no trouble, and no conflict. Worry, care, and responsibility were unknown. In this Utopian World, with everything mine, I was the Monarch, but I was conscious of being alone. A feeling of loneliness and a sense of insecurity took possession of me. I felt a burning desire for something not there. What was it? What did this Utopian World lack? It lacked human beings. There was no one to influence, no one to appreciate, no one to love, and no one to share. Human interest was lacking. In this Utopian World I found myself in a state of misery. A loud knock came on the door. I was thrilled to awake and be conscious of a world filled with people, a place where human beings can attract and be attracted.

Has it ever occurred to you why the ocean is constantly moving up and down with the waves rolling and breaking against each other with clocklike regularity? Without these incessant ups and downs, the ocean would become stagnant. Everything in and around it would perish. These movements keep the water teeming with wholesomeness and vitality.

"A lifetime of happiness! No man alive could bear it; it

185

would be hell on earth," said George Bernard Shaw. The sweet is hidden in the bitter.

How You Can Apply Science to Human Relations

Ups and downs in human nature are a tonic to provoke thoughts and to stimulate action. The World is a proving ground. The people in it furnish a laboratory for the study of human relations. Your ability is the head chemist to compound formulas, and if these are scientifically compounded, you can attract and get what you want. In this chapter, there are formulas compounded in the laboratory of human relations, tested in the field of experience, and proved on the proving grounds of hard knocks.

Einstein's Law of Relativity is abstract until we begin to understand its principle. To understand this principle we find that this obscure scientific law is as close to us as our elbows. According to this law, there is only one kind of material in the Universe, and it is all held together by the Law of Attraction. In physics you were taught that the Law of Attraction is a force acting mutually between particles of matter, tending to draw them together.

The Law of Attraction operates in human relations. It is the formula, the process, the method, and the act you employ to attract people. The more you know about people and the sources that control their acts, the more quickly you can attract them. The formula to do this is a combination of science and art. Science instructs what to do. Art teaches how to do it. Through observation, experience, reflection, and reason you can analyze people. You can uncover reasons that influence and motivate them to act.

People are influenced and motivated into action by ideas. Compounding ideas into a scientific formula and presenting them in logical sequence are the quickest ways to stimulate a reaction and the best means to get results. Human nature is fundamental. There is nothing easier to predict than the reaction you will get from people when you present them with a certain definite idea. A positive idea in action always produces a reaction. This reaction will be favorable if the formula to convey the idea is scientifically prepared.

Over two thousand years ago, Socrates, the wise old Greek, said: "Know thyself." Sometimes a knowledge of ourselves, and what appeals to us gives us a definite clue to what appeals to and attracts others. We discover an appeal that makes people act. Most people are fundamentally alike. What will appeal to one will appeal to all. Most of us are constantly and eternally trying to persuade and even convince ourselves that we are different from everyone else. With forty years' experience working and experimenting in the laboratory of human relations, I know differently. We all have a lot in common with each other. The sooner we realize this, the sooner we will generate the power to attract. We must realize and appreciate one great fact about other people. They are all rational human beings. They have desires, problems, and needs; and they listen to an appeal on how to meet and fulfill them, based on reason and common sense.

The qualities, characteristics, and attributes of other people can usually be determined by an understanding of our own. As Emerson once said: "To speak what other men think, to express what other men feel, is the essence of genius." Therefore, with this understanding, using other people and their needs as the center of interest, we can build and construct thoughts, plans, systems, suggestions, and formulas that will impel them to act. We can attract them and inspire them to have confidence in our proposition.

In analyzing people, we find their acts are controlled by three sources. These three sources were discussed in Chapter 16, "How to Turn Your Ideas into Money." Ideas are the subtle power we employ to attract and to motivate. So important are these sources that I again enumerate them. By all means initiate them in your activities. They are:

1. Emotion

Emotion is the means to send out thoughts to attract attention. Make it easy for people to listen to what you have to say.

2. Judgment

The Judgment is reached through knowledge. You must organize your knowledge and arrange it in sequence. This organization conveys the power of your intelligence and impresses others with what you are capable of doing.

3. Desire

Desire creates the urge to act. To gain attention, and to get interest is not enough. With a feeling of confidence and earnestness, you must arouse the desire, incite that inward, invisible intensity of being, and make others want to do what you propose.

After uncovering the sources that control the acts of people, you must uncover the causes that prompt these sources. These causes are motivated by interests.

What are these interests? There are many, but the three main interests in the lives of most people are:

First: Family.
Second: Vocation or Business.
Third: Themselves.

Practically everything people do in life is centered around one of these interests.

In making an analysis of the causes and the interests to attract people, we discover that these may be influenced by certain advantages, and the effect they have on the lives of people. These advantages are:

First: Gain of happiness or peace of mind.
Second: Gain of health.
Third: Gain of money or wealth.

Thus you have a direct road to the source, a direct road to the cause, and also a road map of the advantages to attract any human being in the world. You have a psychological background that is your foundation.

With this scientific knowledge and information about people, you can create thoughts and plans that will attract people; and, by getting them to believe in you, you can get anything you want. However, if your plans are to succeed, you must believe completely in the things you want and circumscribe these wants with service to others.

Rules Attracting Others

The Law of Attraction is very plainly expressed in the Bible. It reads: "To him that hath shall be given, and from him that hath not shall be taken away even that which he hath." As applied to attracting people, this simply means that if you have the thoughts and forces to attract, and give them out, then you attract other things to you and more things shall be given to you. On the other hand, if you do not make use of the thoughts and forces you now have, then even that which you already have shall be taken away. It merely expresses an inexorable and immutable law that you have got to give to get.

In life you have only one thing to give and that is your ability reviewed and appraised by your own intelligence, and conveyed to others through a system or plan of action. You can give this in a haphazard way, or you can give it in a scientific way. To attract and get what you want, the latter is imperative.

The perfection of a business, art, or profession starts with you. How high do you register in the scale of perfection? What are you doing to improve your efficiency? Have you learned to harness all your forces and concentrate them on the job at hand? Have you acquired the knowledge and skill to do the greatest amount of work with the least possible amount of effort, in the shortest period of time? Can you get maximum results with minimum effort? Are your thoughts liquid? Can you adjust yourself quickly? Have you the power of adaptability? Can you apply common sense? Do you need a slide rule to multiply two by two? Do you assume the role of self-importance when shouldered with the responsibility of directing others? Does your expert knowledge and keen executive ability lose its charm and savor at the expense of impudence and arrogance? Do you use your head for other things, as well as for a place to hang your hat?

How to Capitalize Your Personality

In analyzing and studying the chapters in this book, you realize that the whole purpose of it has been to develop the physical, mental, and spiritual attributes, and to lay a foundation for personal efficiency. It is time to capitalize your personality, and turn your ability into cash. The potentialities are stored up within. How can you connect them with the task at hand? How can you render an efficient service to others?

All social and economic progress comes from individual effort. Economy and society are reflected by you. Energy, ideas, and freedom of action have made America the richest nation in the world. The chief purpose of all business is to fill in with the material things that ideas formulate. Economy is only a distribution of ideas and energy expressed in things to serve and make people happy and comfortable. New ideas, or old ideas with a new body, new knowledge, and new skill, of how to do things better, are always in demand. A need today was only a visualization yesterday, and what is a need today may be only an antique tomorrow.

About seventy-five years ago an old gentleman was about to take out a patent on a certain gadget. On discovering that his proposed patent bore number one hundred thousand, he decided to proceed no further. He took the gadget home, convinced that everything was patented. Since that time several million patents have been taken out, and more than one hundred new ones are going through the Patent Office every day.

Five Rules that Govern Business

All business transacted is built around five general principles. (1) Things needed. The business of food, clothing, and shelter; and also running the Government including the Federal, State, and Municipal, are examples. (2) Things wanted. New ideas create new wants, and to supply these wants man develops new enterprises. This principle includes all businesses to supply the utilities of comfort and enjoyment. Automobiles, household appliances, certain building developments, railroads, steamships, buses, and all time-saving devices are examples. (3) Things to make money. Banks, investment houses, stock exchanges, mortgage companies, underwriting syndicates, investment management, and all business pertaining to finance are examples. (4) Things to satisfy pride. All garments of style, cosmetics, beauty parlors, hairdressing establishments, gift shops, and all things to adorn, are examples. (5) Things to satisfy caution. Man is a cautious creature and he likes to make sure about the future comfort and enjoyment of his family and himself. To secure this he associates himself with others to form a co-operative association for the mutual protection of each other in time of need. The insurance business is an example.

All these different principles of business are conducted by and participated in by human beings. Everyone is endeavoring to serve the other, in order to be served. The better they serve, the better are they served. Therefore, for you to get your share of these goods things, you must evolve a formula to share your good things with others.

How You Can Govern the Five Rules of Business

The highway to the average man's interest is through one of these five principles of business. You have access to this highway and a choice to operate in any of them. You have a definite contribution to make and a definite service to render. Your ability and power as an individual must be expressed through ideas. You must be able to merchandise these ideas, either by creating something new or by improving something old. Every occupation is a merchandising proposition. The person performing that occupation is turning over what he has in order to get something else. In short, he is selling something.

How can you merchandise your ideas?

First: Select the idea you want to accomplish.

Second: Define and enumerate the idea in terms of service, and visualize its values and advantages in concrete terms.

Third: Arrange the idea and its advantage in sequence and give it a solid plan or body. Review Chapter 15 and apply its contents.

Fourth: Idealize the plan; see and feel it attracting attention and getting results. Reinforce your power to do this by the four laws, namely, the law of faith, the law of imagination, the law of repetition, and the law of persistence.

Fifth: Have the plan typewritten in plain words or have a blueprint made if it is to portray a thing. This will make you plan mean something to you and to others.

How to Use the Power of Attraction in Seeking a Job

In applying for a new job or position, review your ideas in the light of your own experience, setting forth in detail past performances, present engagements, and what you feel capable of doing. The employer can react only on what you tell him. Leave nothing to chance. Be thorough and explicit. No one has a better idea of what you are capable of doing and no one can tell it better than you.

Applying the above principles to merchandise his ability, a young fellow presented his qualifications to his next-door neighbor. He specified his training, gave a complete review of his experience, enumerated his attributes and qualities, visualized and idealized his capabilities, and graphically portrayed how the corporation could use and benefit from his services. His next-door neighbor was the president of the corporation. He was so impressed with the plan presenting the young man's work specifications that he immediately employed him at a substantial salary. Today he is vice-president of the corporation.

To try my own prowess, using this plan to merchandise my own ability, I applied to a company for a job. No one in the company knew me. I had no letter of recommendation. I addressed my communication to the president of the company. In brief, I stated my name, age, education, and experience. I enumerated all the different departments of this business from the time the raw material was received until the product was in the hands of the consumer. I visualized in my application all the ins and outs of getting this product to the customer. I suggested a merchandising plan that would make every customer a salesman to obtain a wider distribution of the company's product. I presented a plan that would create and develop a better relation between the customer and the product. I made the president feel that I could increase the business of the company. A few days later I received a letter from him, suggesting an interview to make arrangements for employment at a substantial salary. Of course I did not accept. I called on him as a matter of courtesy and told him of my experiment. He insisted that I take a fee, which I refused.

I did not approach the president of that company begging for a job. I approached him with an idea that meant money to his company. I attracted his attention, incited his interest, and made him feel that I had ideas to share. This, in turn, made him feel that he had a profit to share with me.

Most people are so busy scratching in the dirt that they never stop to think of what the dirt is made. They wonder why they do not get ahead. Now and then one pauses, thinks and analyzes the dirt. He becomes a creative thinker. He uses his head, and the minute he begins to use his head, at that minute he begins to get ahead.

Three men were working on a construction force. Someone asked: "What are you doing?" Number One answered: "I am cutting stone."

Number Two answered: "I am earning $10 a day."

Number Three answered: "I am building a Cathedral."

Number Three has vision and imagination. He is thinking about that which he is doing. Eventually Number Three will be conducting his own business.

Feeling his seniority rights had been overlooked, an employee went to the president of the company to complain that a younger man had been advanced to a position to which he felt entitled. "Why has my twenty-five years of experience been ignored?" he queried. The president said: "You have had only one year's experience twenty-five times."

Merely putting in hours does not win a promotion. It is injecting your ability in the hours that wins recognition and guarantees a reward. Experience is the knowledge, wisdom, and skill gained through a wise use of time.

Use Your Spare Time to Promote Your Success

The use you make of spare time will assist you in developing your ability. There are twenty-four hours in each day. Each week has one hundred and sixty-eight hours. Your vocation takes up forty hours. This leaves you with one hundred and twenty-eight hours each week to sleep, to eat, to entertain, to relax and to improve yourself. By using only 10 per cent of this spare time, you have almost two hours per day to read, to study, to think, to meditate, to reflect, and to improve your capacity to perform. A few hours each week wisely used will enrich your knowledge, broaden your outlook, season your experience and qualify you for a promotion, or an increase in salary. Efficiency and understanding of your job bring added remuneration.

Spare time may be organized effectively. To use it constructively is both interesting and profitable. Decide now to make use of it. Work up a program to use it and adhere to it.

Spare time, either to develop a hobby, an avocation, or self-knowledge, helps to form good habits. Spare time is your property. One man has as much time as another. No one can deprive you of it. The use you make of it largely determines your progress. Fill each minute with sixty seconds. It is not the days or hours that you waste; it is the precious seconds and minutes. It is the use of these that will make or break you. Take care of the minutes, the hours will take care of themselves, and the days will take care of you.

Here are six suggestions that will help you to develop your spare time:

1. Try to spend one hour each day in silent meditation. Read, reflect and review.

2. Pick out one subject, take pencil and paper and write down every thought you can think about on that subject. Spend twenty to thirty minutes each day doing this.

3. Write a letter. Try not to use the words "I," "me," "my" and "mine."

4. Try to converse at least fifteen minutes each day without using the words "I," "me," "my," and "mine."

5. Try to write a little article each day, either explaining, relating, or defining something.

6. Spend at least fifteen minutes each day reviewing and analyzing your experience. Endeavor to visualize and idealize all your relationships with people in a spirit of gratitude and appreciation. It will help you to discover other people's interests. It will help you to form ideas that are wonderful to others because your ideas will make them feel wonderful.

A piece of glass sparkles more brilliantly than a piece of magnetic iron. There is no comparison as to the quality of attraction. This principle is applicable to human relations. It is a simple matter to attract people by superficial amenities, but to draw the blood and influence them to act, you must have the power of attraction within. A smile may win attention, but it takes the conscious power of ideas to obtain results. A hyena can smile, but when an employer wants something done, he does not employ a hyena. The moral is, do not spend all your time painting the outside of the house, but spend more time on the furnishings. It is here you can make people feel at home, and inspire them to do your own bidding.

How to Use the Power of Praise

Someone has said: "Praise is like a diamond. It derives its value from its scarcity."

Praise is one of the greatest motivating forces to attract people. In the Bible is a very vivid story that illustrates the great power of praise. Paul and Silas were unjustly accused, and were cast into prison without trial. It did not daunt their spirits. At midnight they prayed and sang praises to God. An earthquake came. The prison doors opened. Paul and Silas were free men.

In the physical world, there are two ways to expand things:

1. By pressure.
2. By heat.

To expand things elastic, like an automobile tire, air is blown into it or water is poured into it, and the force of pressure of either of these elements expands it.

The inherent pressure from within will expand things when heat is applied. Water is converted to steam, and the steam produces power. Metals are heated to a molten state, and while in this state they can be shaped to any form. Heat applied to coal releases rich gases, coal tar products for dyes, and other useful products, even nylon hosiery.

In the world of human relations, it is not possible to apply physical pressure or heat to individuals. Another formula must be prescribed. The one formula that will aid you more than all others to expand and grow in your relationships with people is the heat of Praise.

Jesus taught and demonstrated Praise. Five thousand hungry people stood before him. Five loaves and two fishes were the only available food. What did he do? He did not complain. He did not grumble. He blessed the five loaves and two fishes. He thanked God for them. He praised them. The whole multitude was fed, and many baskets were left over.

As the father of four children, I endeavor at all times to praise their efforts in a spirit of true appreciation. It works. It seems to tap a hidden fountain within and makes them more eager and alert.

It seems to be an inherent law that we increase whatever we praise. Creation expands to praise. Praise a dog and he is your friend. Praise children and they will glow with joy. Praise plants, flowers, and trees and they will grow better. Praise your ability with gratitude and you increase the flow of intelligence.

Children like praise. Animals like praise, plants like praise, and so do you and I. A little sincere pat on the back increases good will and in many cases contributes to the success and happiness of others. Positive praise feelingly applied is an active prayer. Practice it.

Whatever we praise multiplies. If you are in need of supply, the best way to start the flow of additional supplies is to praise that which you have. If you want a better job and more pay, start praising the work you are doing. Those around you may seem unappreciative, but keep praising your situation and soon they will be thinking your way. You will be amazed how quickly things begin to turn your way.

William Law once wrote: "If anyone could tell you the shortest, surest way to all happiness and all perfection, he must tell you to thank and praise God for everything that happens to you. For it is certain that whatever seeming calamity happens to you, if you thank and praise God for it, you turn it into a blessing. Could you, therefore, work miracles, you could not do more for yourself than by this thankful spirit; for it turns all that it touches into happiness."

Praise magnifies the good qualities, and minimizes the bad ones—if any. Praise is a positive expression of appreciation. It is being glad over the accomplishments of others. It is something you can't buy. It must be earned, and shared by those who deserve it. It is more than fame and money. It is giving hearty and warm approval to a friend. It is letting him know that you are interested in his welfare. It breaks down barriers and lets you in on situations that would not otherwise be possible. Praise may be called the Great Liberator. Therefore, when anyone deserves or earns your approbation, by all means give it—now. You will encourage them and have a greater appreciation of your own qualities.

Do Ordinary Things in an Extraordinary Way

People stop learning too soon. They reach the mature age of thirty and think they can learn no longer. Learn something new, formulate new ideas, develop new interests, and generate new enthusiasm. In these you will find new zest, new courage, and new inspiration to perfect your job. Ordinary things done in an extraordinary way attract more attention and create more interest than extraordinary things done in an ordinary way. It is not necessary to be an economic royalist to have stars in your crown, friends among your associates, and money in your pocket.

Two of my good friends are Frederick Beckhusen and Karl Kaltenhauser. They are head masseurs at Young's Health Institute. Two finer characters could not be found. These two men know the names, characteristics, idiosyncrasies, and personal attributes of over three thousand men. Every member at Young's Health Institute loves and respects these men. Why? Because these men do ordinary things in an extraordinary way. They give their best willingly and cheerfully at all times. They are able to attract and get what they want.

Speaking of being too old to learn, take a lesson from Moses. According to the Bible, Moses was eighty years old when he started his great work. He led the Children of Israel out of Egyptian bondage, and incorporated the Ten Commandments through the inspiration and guidance of God. After forty years of stewardship, leading, and directing the Israelites, we find Moses at the ripe young age of one hundred and twenty, with a clear eye and a steady hand.

In attracting people it is not wise to rely too much on education. Intelligence precedes education. Man had intelligence long before he acquired education. Education comes from the Latin word "educare," which means "to draw out." The whole process of education is to draw out and develop the latent abilities and to arrange them according to the standard of convention, that others may understand and benefit by them.

How to Uncover the Universal Laws of Consciousness

The human consciousness is a product of God. It is created and formed in harmony with order. Even though it is not recognized, law and order prevail in the human consciousness, and anyone skilled in the knowledge and understanding of human relations forms ideas on this hypothesis.

To have the maximum effect, any medium to exchange or to transmit thoughts and ideas must follow this principle. Order glorifies the principle of God, and harmonizes with the cosmic consciousness which operates throughout the Universe, and in the consciousness of man.

I can make as much sound on the piano as Iturbi. Iturbi, through science, knowledge, and skill, arranges those sounds with the keys of the piano to form a sound pattern. This sound pattern harmonizes with the order of the Universe to produce the concord of sweet sound, which is music. This principle applies to ideas. To attract and influence they must be formed into a pattern with the right words, and arranged in harmony with order.

In the Universe, there is nothing supernatural. All things are governed by the immutable and unchangeable Law of God. God is Truth. Why? Because Truth is an established principle with no exceptions. All natural laws are principles of God.

The law of physics, the law of mathematics and the law of chemistry are, have been, and always will be Truths. All of these laws are an established principle with no exception. Two parts of hydrogen and one of oxygen made water before man wrote the chemical formula H_2O. Two parts added to two more parts made four parts before man discovered mathematics. An apple was falling to the ground the day before Newton discovered the Law of Gravitation. Electricity was available to light the Egyptian Pyramids, but the Egyptians did not know how to cut the lines of force, set up a magnetic field, and use a dynamo to convert physical force into electrical energy. An airplane flown over Bethlehem the day Jesus was born would have been considered a miracle. Yet the principle of aerodynamics was as applicable then as it is now.

The Law of God is not based on chance. "Chance is a word void of sense and nothing can exist without cause," said Voltaire. So-called luck is based on chance. If what Voltaire says is true, then luck can play no part in obtaining results. Achievement must have a cause. Accomplishments are not pulled out of the air. They are the results attained by the application of ideas in well-formed plans, loaded with fact, meaning, and feeling centered around the needs of people conforming to the Law of God, which is the principle of Good.

How to Find Order in Life's Relationships

Another thought that will help you to attract and get what you want is to recognize and realize that all branches of knowledge teach relationship. Everything in the Universe is related. To be conscious of this fact and demonstrate it with kindness and appreciation toward all things is to have all the forces of the Universe co-operating with you. Man can multiply two by two, or he can divide two into two from now until the end of time. This proves that man is a part of the infinite, and also is a part of the infinitesimal. I know that I am a part of everything in the Universe, and that everything in the Universe is a part of me. I work on this principle. Feeling that I am a unit in the Universe and a citizen of the world brings me in contact with harmony and unity. I am at home in the kitchen or the drawing room. Man worries because he does not know. Man dreads because he does not understand. Man fails because he does not think. When you love God, you love Good, and this establishes order in your relationships that produces unity and what you do is done with certainty and harmony. This is Peace of Mind.

"Know ye the Truth and the Truth shall make you free."

In all your relations, endeavor to discover what is true, and practice what is good. Believe in yourself, and acquire the habits that will make you believe in yourself. Act as if it were impossible to fail. Keep active. Genius is 1 per cent inspiration and 99 per cent perspiration. Geniuses are only people who keep busy in the perfection of a science or an art. Longfellow knew this when he wrote:

> The heights by great men reached and kept
> Were not attained by sudden flight.
> But they, while their companions slept,
> Were toiling upward in the night.

Remember these few precepts.

(1) Get the attitude of success; think and feel it. A flower girl of London looked like a duchess, thought like a duchess, talked like a duchess, acted like a duchess, and soon became a duchess in the play "Pygmalion."

(2) Operate scientifically. Know all the facts. No business is good enough for a man to spend a day in, but any business is good enough for him to spend a lifetime in. The road to perfection is not crowded.

(3) An automobile performs better in nigh gear, so does your personality. Throw it in gear and go places and do things.

(4) Be cheerful. Smile, but do not depend upon it for an increase in salary.

(5) Keep flexible. Changes are taking place with lightning rapidity. Learn to adapt yourself quickly to conditions and adjust yourself gracefully to people.

(6) Study people, find out what they like, and make plans to supply them.

(7) Exercise tact and diplomacy. Feel your way along. It is better to get there whole than in parts.

(8) Agree with thine adversary quickly. The storm does not last very long.

(9) Be forgiving. Next time it may be on you.

(10) Speak softly. Arrogance and impudence have their reward.

(11) Be dependable. If you make an appointment or an agreement, keep it. Let your word be your bond.

(12) Think, then act, and you will not grow weary acting. The more you think, the less work you have to do.

(13) Be a friend. The only way to have a friend is to be one. Execute all your ideas with a humble and friendly spirit.

(14) If you feel the symptoms of self-importance, and a slight attack of big-headedness coming on, take this antidote. "Think of all things that have been done, all things that are being done, and all things that will be done, even without you and me."

Your Ideas Bring Results

Keep planting ideas. Some will fall upon stony hearts, some will fall upon marble domes, but some will fall upon fertile brains and will bring forth some thirty, some sixty, and some even a hundredfold of good results. The Law of Averages is a very exacting law. It requires that you plant ideas, but it never fails to reward you justly. When you have earned something, nothing in the Universe will keep you from getting it.

You can attract and get what you want by simply believing in your ideas. They are the substance of things you want; and if you have faith in them, the substance of the ideas becomes the evidence of the things you wanted. Every successful achievement has followed this principle.

In this chapter I have revealed to you the psychological attributes and the spiritual qualities that enable you to attract people, and impel them to be conscious of your ideas. Ideas that conform to a pattern are like music to the ear; they inspire confidence and motivate action by virtue of their own power. They are the very essence of business. They are irresistible. People feel about them the way you feel. You can build and create ideas around the needs of others that will attract attention, stimulate the imagination, wake up the slumbering interest, electrify the latent desires, incite the feeling, and move people to action. Your ability to attract and get what you want in yourself does lie. Use it and results will follow as the night the day.

Chapter 22

HOW THE LAW OF AVERAGES CAN MAKE YOU RICH

Love is the Universal Law of Justice. That is why God is Love. All natural laws express justice. Natural laws have no favorites, and are available to all who endeavor to understand and apply them. The Law of Averages is a natural law. It works with all and for all with absolute certainty, precision, and justice.

Man in his quest for knowledge uncovers many natural laws. He reduces these laws to workable things, and through the effects of these laws is able to add to his own comfort and enjoyment. He is able to prove the effects of these laws, and to express them in scientific formulas. The Law of Averages can be reduced to a scientific formula, and applied in dealing with people. The results may be anticipated with accuracy. In my forty years of experience in the field of selling, I have proved that the Law of Averages applies to human beings as well as to things. A scientific knowledge of the Law of Averages is one of the most stimulating and fascinating factors in business. The application of this law guarantees success in any field of endeavor.

In this chapter I want to give you--First: A practical introduction that proves the Law of Averages in dealing with things and people. Second: I want to give you a scientific interpretation of the Law of Averages. Third: I want to tell you how the Law of Averages can make you rich and also how it works with me and for me.

How the Law of Averages Works

To introduce the scientific application of the Law of Averages let us observe a demonstration. Take a coin and toss it into the air one hundred times. Mark down the number of times it falls heads, and the number of times it falls tails. What happens? There are two sides to that coin, and both sides are exposed. The Law of Averages determines the number of times that the coin falls heads and the number of times that it falls tails. As there are only two sides exposed, it must fall an equal number of times heads, and also an equal number of times tails. A coin tossed into the air a sufficient number of times will get the same result every time.

There is another demonstration that will interest you. Number ten golf balls, one, two, three and right on up to ten. Put them in a sack and shake them thoroughly. Draw one. The number you draw is one of the ten. The Law of Averages yields number one every time during the ten draws Draw these balls one hundred times, and during the draws the Law of Averages yields the ball marked number one and two in succession. Draw these balls one thousand times, and during the draws the Law of Averages yields the balls marked number one, two and three in succession. Draw these balls ten thousand times, and during the draws the Law of Averages yields the balls marked number one, two, three, and four in succession. Draw these balls one hundred thousand times, and during the draws the Law of Averages yields the balls marked one, two, three, four and five in succession. Keep the draws up to ten billion, and during the draws the Law of Averages yields the balls marked one, two, three, four, five, six, seven, eight, nine and ten in succession. If you do not believe it, try it.

Either of the above demonstrations will prove that the Law of Averages works. Since it does work, let us endeavor to define it. Socrates, one of the greatest thinkers who ever lived, had one great motto: "Define your terms." It is only logical, therefore, that you should know the scientific meaning of the Law of Averages. In my attempt to define the Law of Averages, I wrote letters, made inquiries, and asked many questions. From these different sources I received many ideas and suggestions. To sum them all up the answer was: "If you put something in, you get something out." A very good answer and it contains the elements of truth. However, it did not satisfy me.

Many millions of people had seen things fall to the ground long before Sir Isaac Newton discovered the Law of Gravitation. But Newton wanted to know the reason why things fell to the ground. Someone asked him how he discovered the Law of Gravitation. His answer was: "By thinking about it."

After thinking many days about the Law of Averages in terms of application, in terms of demonstration, in terms of relationships, and in terms of how it produces results, I created the following definition.

The Law of Averages is the law that determines the number of times a thing will happen in proportion to the number of times that that thing is exposed.

The coin is exposed one hundred times. It has two sides only, heads and tails. Therefore, it must fall an equal number of times for each side and will always do this in proportion to the number of times it is exposed. The same principle applies to the golf balls. Expose them enough times and the result you are seeking is bound to happen.

How to Use the Law of Averages

The definition of the Law of Averages establishes it on a scientific basis. Therefore, it will prove very helpful to you to visualize this definition, and get it well established in your mind. To know a principle thoroughly inspires us to apply it. Anyone who applies the Law of Averages based on the above definition cannot fail to produce results.

Some may confuse the Law of Averages with chance. Chance comes from the Latin word "cadere" which means "to fall." Chance is taking a gamble that a thing will happen. It is a pure risk with a possibility to win based on that imaginary thing called luck. The Law of Averages is a definite law that eliminates chance, avoids risk, and fulfills every requirement to which it is applied.

The Law of Averages is used by all life insurance companies to determine the death rate of a given number of people at a given age. It is the scientific principle on which to compute all mortality tables. Why? Because a given number of people are exposed to death at all times, and therefore, a certain number of deaths will happen each year, with absolute accuracy. This fact, plus the rate of interest earned on the premiums collected, determines the cost of the life insurance per year.

The Law of Averages also applies to the investment portfolio. Out of a given number of companies doing business, a certain number of these companies will be successful. A financial institution can invest in a sufficient number of these companies in order that the Law of Averages can operate. This provides a reasonable security for an investment and also a guaranteed interest return on the investment. Therefore, by applying the Law of Averages, a financial institution can invest money scientifically.

Most credit risks are based on the Law of Averages. Out of a given number of credit risks, a certain number will always be responsible and prove to be satisfactory.

In all enterprises the Law of Averages operates. Some people in business are conscious of this law, and expand their enterprises with speed, alacrity, and certainty. Others apply it in a hit or miss fashion, but they by no means reap the rich and full reward of its scientific application.

"Ignorance of the law excuseth no man"—is an old legal maxim applying to the law of the land. To commit a crime with the plea of ignorance does not excuse the offender. The same principle applies to the laws of creation, except these laws are more exacting. To be ignorant of these laws in no way interferes with their operation. The laws are here for us to use and not to use them is certainly no fault of the laws. The Law of Averages is a fundamental law of creation. To apply it is to enjoy its rewards.

The Law of Averages is expressed no less than three times in the Bible—in the thirteenth chapter of Matthew, the fourth chapter of Mark, and the eighth chapter of Luke. In each of these different chapters is found the "Parable of the Sower," which plainly states that the Sower must sow his seed before he can expect to reap a crop. Some seed will fall by the wayside; some will fall among thorns; some will fall among the rocks; but some will fall upon good ground and bring forth a crop of a hundredfold.

The secret of the Sower is the kind of seed that he sows. The seed must be of good quality in order to take root when it falls on the right soil. That which he reaps will be of the same nature as that which he sows. If he sows wind, he will reap a whirlwind. If he sows sawdust he will reap sawdust. Everything increaseth after its own kind. As the seed contains all the elements essential to the plant, so must ideas contain all the elements essential to influence people. You must sow ideas before you can reap a reward. You must give before you can get. So when you sow and when you give, do it freely with no strings to it. As Jesus put it, "Except a kernel of wheat fall into the ground and die, it abideth alone. But if it die, it beareth much fruit." You do your part and the seed will do its part.

Most of us, most of the time, are thwarted, distracted, and discouraged because we have no definite knowledge of a law on which to expand our efforts. Doubt, uncertainty, and dread creep into our consciousness, and there is a tendency to vacillate from one goal to another, from one interest to another, and we end up by being simply bewildered with a shallow sense of being cheated. In applying a fundamental law, be not anxious or overzealous to change your procedure. Remember that natural laws do not vacillate. The laws that rule the Universe are unchangeable. They unfold logically. Observe how logically things in nature grow and develop. Nothing is accidental. They develop in logical sequence and unfold in perfect fruition.

The Laws of God cannot fail. To fail would be a violation of God's own principles. This is impossible. Does the Law of Gravitation fail? Drop what you have in your hand and see what happens. This law is constantly on the job even though you are not conscious of it. The Law of Physics, the Law of Chemistry, the Law of Mathematics, or any other fundamental law is constantly available for our use. Someone may ask what a dozen eggs will cost at 6 cents each. Instantly, through the Law of Mathematics, you multiply 12 x 6 and solve the problem. The moment you are conscious of the Law, it is there to meet your need.

Thus far, I have given you a practical demonstration of the

Law of Averages. I have defined it and have endeavored to interpret it scientifically. From here on I want to show how the Law of Averages works for you and for me.

How the Law of Averages Can Work for You and Me

The Law of Averages yields results with the same certainty and accuracy as the Law of Mathematics, when applied. I not only believe in the Law of Averages, I not only have faith in it, but more than these, I know the Law of Averages operates. When I multiply 6 x 12 I know it is 72. Faith and belief in the Law of Mathematics become ready knowledge. The application of the Law of Averages becomes ready and usable knowledge the minute it is applied.

Not many years ago, I made 1800 calls over the telephone. I did not get a bite. Was I dismayed? Was I frustrated? Was I discouraged? Not in the least. I was exposing an idea in the form of a sales plan portraying the benefits of life insurance. I was putting into operation the Law of Averages. I knew that this Law could not fail. Operating on this principle, there was no occasion for doubt. I knew that results were certain. What happened? Within a few days, I struck the jackpot. It rained business. Did the Law of Averages pay off? In less than one month I received more than $2.00 for every telephone call made. In addition, I received a bonus of at least that much more.

In the field of selling, the Law of Averages is very exacting as to the amount of calls necessary for a sale. It certainly requires that you plant ideas, but it does not prescribe the method to use. In fact, the Law of Averages is absolutely indifferent as to the method you employ to put it in operation. In my experience in selling, I have always used the telephone. I find that the telephone method is the quickest, the most practical, the most efficient, the most feasible, and the most scientific method of carrying an idea to the greatest number of people in the shortest period of time. It is the quickest and most direct means of exposing an idea in a personalized way and, therefore, fulfilling the requirements necessary for the Law of Averages to operate.

In applying the Law of Averages in the field of selling, it is absolutely necessary to determine the result you desire. The Law of Averages does not know the objective you desire until the decision is made. Once a decision is reached, the law goes into operation to fulfill it. The number of times you expose an idea about a product or service is the number that determines how often the exposition of that idea will reward you.

Most of the people who sell work either on a commission basis or for a salary. If you work on a commission basis, put a definite cash value on each call. If you work on a salary, put a definite estimate of the number of calls you want to make to consummate a sale. Keep a record and watch the Law of Averages operate.

In my own experience, I have always placed a value of $2.00 on each telephone call. Therefore, if I make 50 telephone calls in one day, I know I have earned $100.00. To illustrate this fact, it will be of interest to you to know that in June 1947 I began to operate the Law of Averages on this basis. At the end of December 1947, I found that I had made 3,000 telephone calls and the Law of Averages paid me not only $2.00 for each call, but again rewarded me with a substantial bonus.

You may ask, "Does the Law of Averages work among strangers?" Does the sun know any strangers? The Law of Averages knows no strangers, and once it is put in operation it works like a magnet. It attracts and draws to it the thing you desire. Remember the "Parable of the Sower," always rely upon good seed. The value and advantage of the product, or service, and what they mean to the prospect, are the seed you sow. To expose ideas built into a sales plan and transmit them with absolute faith and certainty to a given number of prospects puts the Law of Averages in operation. Are reactions to ideas predictable? Yes, there is nothing more certain to predict than the reaction you will get from a given number of people when you present them with a certain definite idea. A positive action always gets a reaction. This reaction will be favorable or unfavorable. If it is favorable, you act upon it quickly. If it is unfavorable, you forget it and go after another one.

Are you seeking a job? Do you want a larger salary? Do you want to improve your present occupation? Apply the Law of Averages and it can be a decided advantage to bring about any of the above situations. How can this be achieved? Formulate ideas about what you want to accomplish. Begin to apply these ideas. Keep on trying. Be convinced that the Law of Averages is working with you and through the process of elimination is helping you to reach your goal. Therefore, by persistence your efforts will be crowned with achievement, and what you are seeking will automatically manifest itself in your experience.

In applying the Law of Averages, endeavor to be patient. Shake the limb of an apple tree with a green apple upon it, and nothing happens. Shake the limb when the apple is ripe and the apple falls off. Also remember the grain—"first the blade, then the ear, and then the full grain in the ear." The Law of Averages cannot be forced, coerced, or hastened. When the requirements are met, it operates with precision. Nothing can force it to act, and nothing can prevent it from acting.

The Law of Averages will remunerate you in proportion to the value you yourself put on it. If you demand little, it pays little. If you demand much and set a worth-while goal, it will always meet your standard. The old saying goes, "Why put a mountain in labor, just to bring forth a mouse?"

Tell the Law of Averages what you want. Ask for it, seek it, and demand it in a humble and sincere way—then stick to that demand with faith, with persistence and determination until you have achieved your objective.

N. W. Ayer, one of the greatest advertising men that this country ever produced, had a great slogan: "Keeping everlastingly at it brings success." Some people think that this implies a form of slavery. I think possibly Mr. Ayer was referring to the Law of Averages. A chain of ideas puts into operation the Law of Averages and brings about results. An idea once in print begins to accelerate a process of other ideas, to form a chain of influence, and eventually through the Law of Averages the idea brings success.

In applying the Law of Averages, remember that you have no control over its rewards or the source from which the rewards come. It rewards you from the most unsuspected sources and in the most unexpected way. As a salesman you may be all aglow with a sure sale. On the surface the prospect could not fail. What happens? The prospect does fail to buy. Why? Because he is human. The Law of Averages, on the other hand, cannot fail, and what you thought only a "suspect" turns into a genuine sale. This principle applies also to those who seek a job, a larger salary, or an improvement in occupation. The reward comes from the source least expected.

The Law of Averages is unlike man-made law. It cannot be changed, altered, or amended. No act of chicanery, no cunning fraud and no art of deception can force it to act, or cause it to fail. It can only be put into action by concentrated thought. The true purpose of the Law of Averages is to give you a definite plan of action with the absolute assurance that the application of your ability cannot fail to produce results. This assurance gives you the power and determination to carry on.

The experiences which I have enumerated are not opinions or theories about the Law of Averages. They are the Law of Averages in action. This Law does not need a favorable place or a favorable time to operate. It will operate for anyone, at any time, or at any place. It requires concentration and application and these provoke quick thinking. Many constructive thoughts and ideas will come to you as you begin to apply the Law of Averages. Your ability to express these thoughts and ideas will increase as you need them. Your knack of applying the Law of Averages will give you many thrills and many checks. It can make you rich.

Chapter 23

HOW TO FIND YOUR PLACE
IN LIFE

The other day while looking over the Sunday paper, my eyes were instantly drawn to a picture of a graduating class at one of the large universities. I analyzed that picture. The faces on those boys appeared to be uncertain, not uncertain about life or its future, but uncertain as to the place they could take in it. They seemed to be in a quandary. Were they wondering where it would be possible for them to fit in? Were they wondering how to make the most efficient use of their talents and abilities to render the best and most useful service?

Are You in the Right Place?

Not only boys graduating from universities and colleges, but thousands of other people are wondering at all times if they are in the right place. Am I a square peg in a round hole, or am I a round peg in a square hole? Am I making the full use of my talents? Are my abilities being channeled in the right directions? Is there not some occupation or thing that I can do more efficiently? Are my efforts being fully appreciated? These are typical questions people ask themselves. Most every one is seeking to find, or to improve, his place in life. He wants a place in the sun, where his knowledge and skill may be applied with

217

efficiency and where unity, harmony, and peace of mind may be enjoyed.

Is there a system or a guide to help people find their true place in life? Is it necessary to stumble hither and yon with no definite objective? After giving this subject much thought, I evolved five steps to help you. Take these five steps and you will be in your place.

1. Take Stock of Your Ability

If you were going to engage in a business, the first sensible and practical thing to do would be to take a complete inventory. You would survey its present location, inspect the building, make an inventory of the stock, appraise the fixtures, list its assets and tabulate its liabilities. You would quietly analyze these data. You would visualize the business in relation to the customer. You would study his needs and wants, and make provision to supply them. Your chief desire would be to render a good service to the customer and to earn a reasonable profit. You would study also the opportunities of the business, work out methods to improve them, and endeavor to realize and to capitalize on its possibilities.

The same principle applies to yourself. You are in a sense a merchant, and your business is to merchandise your ability. When you bought this book, it became your silent partner. By using its contents in conjunction with your business, there is no limit to where you can go.

The central location of your ability is in your occupation. It matters not what it is, or where it is located, it has unlimited possibilities for improvement and expansion.

The building from which you operate is your body. It must be maintained and kept in good condition. It must be well fed and well treated. It supplies the energy with which to perform and gives vitality to the ability. It qualifies you to work with efficiency. Keep it in good condition by applying the principles in Chapter 9, "How to Double Your Energy."

Your stock of goods represents your thoughts. Are you dishing out negative thoughts to drive the customer away? Are you using positive thoughts to increase the business and to fulfill your desires? Read Chapter 1, "It Might Have Been You."

Are you making full use of your stock in the basement? Do you bring it out, let people know what you have? You can draw on your stock in the basement, and make full use of it by reading Chapter 3 "Are You Nine-Tenths Under Water?"

Do you observe the customer's needs? Do you concentrate on methods and plans to satisfy those needs? Have you his name listed correctly and can you recall the last transaction? Do you reason out his wants in advance and contemplate how to take care of them? Do you stir in a little of the Priceless Ingredient every now and then, that he may know your real value and spread your name around among his neighbors? Chapter 5 "How to Increase Your Power to Think and to Build," catalogues all these and tells you how to make the wisest use of them.

Do you use the right words in presenting your stock, in order that the customer may have full confidence and a complete knowledge of what you can do for him? Chapter 11 "The Key to a Fortune" tells how.

Have you enthusiasm for your business, and can you generate it in yourself, and also in the customer? Read Chapter 13 "How to Generate Enthusiasm."

Do you lack faith in your business? Is your stock getting shop-worn and ragged around the edges? Read "The Most Interesting Thing in the World," and watch your business improve.

Are you making the full use of your ideas to improve the stock, stimulate buying interest, and enlarge the business? New ideas about commonplace things often attract attention, and arouse buying interests in the customer. Read "How to Turn Your Ideas into Money," Chapter 16.

Are you anxious about the future of your business? Are you concerned about a shortage in stock? Are you uncertain and doubtful about conditions? Is your peace of mind perturbed? Review Chapter 18 "How to Make Use of the Present."

Have you inspected your fixtures lately? How about your equipment to display your merchandise? Your speech, voice, and manner are the best fixtures you have. A good overhauling will improve them. It will help you to display your stock, and make it easy for the customer to understand and have full confidence in what you say. Review "How to Improve Your Speech, Voice, and Manner," Chapter 17.

You are a good merchant. You have a wonderful reputation. The Rotary Club wants to know how you do it. You are called upon to make a speech. You can do it. Read "How to Make a Speech," Chapter 19.

Do you want more business? Do you want to attract more customers? Do you want people to feel kindly toward you? Do you want to extend your services? Chapter 21, "How to Attract and Get What You Want," tells you how to do it.

Is your merchandise on display at all times? Are you exposing it to the greatest number of people, in order to increase the number of customers? The Law of Averages never fails. Read "How the Law of Averages Can Make You Rich," Chapter 22.

If you take stock of your ability in the light of this analysis, and use the chapters of this book to coach and guide you, you will be a going concern on any corner. You will have unlimited working capital, and a surplus sufficient to weather any storm. Your place in life will be secure.

2. *Practice Self-Reliance*

The other day I took a walk in the woods. I came to a very beautiful tree and plucked a leaf from that tree. I observed its form, its size, its color, and also the many lines running through its body. In symmetry and design, no artist could have imitated its beauty. In texture and construction, no sculptor could have approximated its formation. Every line from stem to tip had its place. It was an expression of perfection, the apex of quality. From the same tree, on a near-by limb, I plucked another leaf. On the tree its appearance was identical with the one that I had just examined. As they hung on the tree it was impossible to tell them apart. However, when I put those leaves side by side, and compared them, I instantly discovered a decided difference. Each leaf was perfect, and each one had its own form, size, color, lines, and what I call its own leaf-ality. I plucked from the same tree a dozen more leaves and, on close analysis, I found each leaf had its own individuality.

I began to study the tree. Very near was another tree. At close range the general appearance of those two trees was almost the same. I walked a few feet away, and looked at those trees. I discovered a decided contrast in their contour. I examined the limbs, the twigs, and the bark of those trees; all bore a striking similarity, and also a striking contrast. The trees, like the leaves from the tree, have an individuality.

The analytical description of the trees and the leaves, establishes one fundamental principle that exemplifies individual self-reliance. Self-reliance bestows on them the power to draw on, and to absorb all the forces around them with a capacity to fulfill a natural law. The appearance of each tree and each leaf indicates a complete fruition of health, harmony, unity, and prosperity.

All animals practice the doctrine of self-reliance. They follow their natural instinct, which is a natural spontaneous impulse of propensity, moving them without reason toward action, essential to their existence, preservation, and development. By adhering to this instinct, they are fed, sustained, and maintained in their natural habitat, and live a complete and full life.

All birds and fowls follow their natural instinct, and they too are fed, nourished and sustained, maintained and directed in what to do and how to do it.

All things in nature practice and demonstrate the power of self-reliance. To observe the acts of plants, trees, birds, fowl, animals, fish, and insects should be an inspiration to every man to practice self-reliance. "Observe the lilies of the fields, they toil not, neither do they spin, and yet Solomon in all his glory is not arrayed like one of these." Observe the robin that built a nest in your backyard, as he goes south in November and returns the following spring to his old nest. Observe the homing pigeon being shipped a thousand miles away from his home. When released without compass or chart, he circles a moment, and then makes a beeline back to his home. Observe the salmon returning after years at sea to the exact river in which he was born. Observe a bee five miles away from its hive (equivalent to one thousand miles for a man) returning laden with its pollen. Observe the horse keeping in the road on the darkest night. Observe the bear hibernating. Observe the dog without map, guide or road sign, scenting his way home a thousand miles away. Do not forget the cell from which you sprang. These are only a few examples. The list is infinite. This must prove that God, the Supreme Intelligence of the Universe, works in and through all things, including man.

God knows His business. He makes no mistakes. Everything created by Him has a place, or it would not have been created. You have a place. You are an individual. Your fingerprints indicate this. Of all the millions of fingerprints on record, no two are alike. Your fingerprints distinguish you. You are a complete entity possessed with all the qualities and attributes to unfold into a perfect individual. You cannot imitate another's fingerprints, and neither can you ape another's ability. You must rely on your own. You must practice self-reliance.

What is self-reliance? It is relying on your own mental resources, judgment, and ability to perform. It is absolute trust in the integrity of your own mind. Integrity is the quality of being complete. It is the independence of individuality and helps you to realize that no part of you can be separated from the whole of you. You have got what it takes at any time or any place. All you have to do is to rely on it. Think, speak, and act your latent convictions and they shall be the means to influence all men. Self-reliance is the power to believe in your own thought, and to act as if it were impossible to fail.

Conventional methods and orthodox procedure are excellent guides, but they are very poor teachers. "That which each can do best, none but his Creator can teach him." In the distance I can hear a woodthrush. The loud, clear notes are an exquisite arrangement of tone and pitch blending into the concord of sweet sound. It is music at its source. I pause. The woodthrush never had a lesson in voice culture. It teaches a lesson on self-reliance.

Situations arise from time to time where it is absolutely necessary to practice self-reliance. Conditions must be met on the spot. You must either sink or swim. I encounter many of these situations in selling by telephone. The following one is a good example.

I called a very prosperous wool merchant on the telephone, whom I had never seen. His secretary answered the telephone and she put me through the third degree as to my name, history, pedigree, business qualifications and last, but not least, she wanted to know what I wanted to talk to Mr. Woolman about. I told her my mission point blank. I told her I was calling Mr. Woolman about a life insurance plan. That positive statement of fact connected me with Mr. Woolman. "Is this Mr. J. Edgar Woolman?" I said. "Yes, what about it?" Then with a mellow but firm voice I told my story. Attentively he listened and when I had finished he said, "I am not interested." I accepted his statement. Self-reliance came in and suggested that I could possibly convince him more thoroughly if I knew his date of birth, and submit my plan in the form of a brief. Believing that discretion is the better part of valor, and that a soft word turneth away wrath, I spoke to him very gently and said: "Mr. Woolman, I have never met you, yet I know you are like all other good businessmen. I know you are naturally a good sport. Therefore, Mr. Woolman, I want you to do me a favor and that favor is simply this: I want you to give me your date of birth." To which he replied, "I do not care to give out my date of birth to a stranger, over the telephone." Self-reliance said: "Mr. Woolman, will you loan me your date of birth for a few days." Laughingly he replied: "August 15, 1905."

In a few days I submitted the plan for Mr. Woolman's consideration. He liked it and as a result of that telephone conversation, using the principle of self-reliance, I sold him a one-hundred-thousand-dollar life-insurance policy.

Man is born with an instinct—the instinct of self-preservation. When he acquired the power of conscious thought, he changed the name of instinct to intuition, but he did not change its source, purpose, quality, or power. Intuition may be defined as a quick perception without conscious attention or reason. It is ready knowledge from within, knowledge that is always available to act in an emergency, to thwart a disaster, or to avert a calamity. I like to think of intuition as the trunk-line of communication directly to God. Often hunches present themselves. Sometimes a hunch tells you what to do instantly.

Following a hunch carries me back thirty years ago. I was traveling in the South selling paint and roofing material. In my territory was a purchasing agent who bought for fifty different cotton mills. I called at his office and a young lady took my card in. A minute later she returned and gave me a nickel for my card. A hunch came. I sent another card in with a message that the cards were two for a nickel. I was going down the corridor and the young lady came shouting after me that Mr. Purchasing Agent wanted to see me. I went in. I told him that I was honest and did not want to cheat him. Following a little hunch, I received an order for several carloads of material.

Self-reliance is one of the fundamental principles of existence. It develops character and will help you to perfect yourself, and to perfect yourself is to perfect your place in life. "To reform a nation, to reform a world, no wise man will undertake and all but foolish men know, the only solid and thorough reformation is what each one begins and perfects in himself."

This may be of interest to you. Take a one-dollar bill and turn the green side up. On the left side of this bill you will observe a pyramid, and just above the pyramid is a triangle, or the unfinished part of the pyramid. Look at the eye glowing out of that triangle. It almost speaks. The eye in the triangle represents the All-Seeing and All-Knowing Eye of God. That triangle represents the apex of perfection. Over the triangle is the Latin phrase "Annuit Coeptis." Translated, this means "God looks on with favor."

That triangle symbolizes the individual dignity of man, and recognizes his individual integrity. That is a traditional heritage that guarantees to every American the right to perfect himself in any art, craft, business, profession, science or in any other field of endeavor. He can rise to the top. This traditiona' heritage is symbolized in the Great Seal of the United States. This means that these individual rights are guaranteed to you by the entire resources of the United States. It is a franchise to encourage everyone to practice self-reliance. This heritage and right should set a man on fire with inspiration. It is a wonderful country where a poor boy can become the head of it.

Always remember what Burroughs, the great naturalist, said about his friend Emerson, the great essayist. "Where he was at all he was all together." It makes the practice of self-reliance a reality.

3. Let Your Light Shine

Have you ever turned on the light in a dark room? It makes a vast difference. Yet nothing has changed. The only thing lacking was light. A little light makes a big difference. It matters not where you are or what you are doing, the minute you light up your consciousness you light up the place around you.

The best way to light up your place in life is to turn on the light of Optimism. Optimism comes from the Latin word "optimus," which means "best." It is looking for the best in everything and everybody.

The optimist is right. The pessimist is right. One sees things in the light. One sees things in the dark. Each is right. They only see things from different points of view. The optimist sees things as they are, and is able to establish their proper relations. The pessimist only sees a small part of things, and is unable to establish their true relationship. The optimist has knowledge enlightened by facts. The pessimist has knowledge but it is dimmed by ignorance. The optimist sees the doughnut, the pessimist sees the hole.

Optimism is thinking straight. It is an excellent vaccine to prevent failure. It is maintaining a sense of equilibrium regardless of what happens. It puts in practice the adage taught by Marcus Aurelius: "Whatever happens at all happens as it should happen."

A man without a penny dropped into a restaurant. He ordered one dozen oysters. He was an optimist. He hoped to find a pearl with which to pay for the oysters. In the last oyster he found a pearl worth one thousand dollars. Does optimism pay?

When you walk toward the light, the shadows are back of you. When you walk away from the light, the shadows are before you. Practice and demonstrate optimism in your affairs. Always walk toward the light and endeavor to encourage others to walk with you. Let your light shine. Trim the wick with kindness, and feed it with the oil of optimism.

Optimism is like digging a hole in the ground, the more you take from it, the larger it gets. You can share it with others, because it is inexhaustible. It is also like a sweet-scented perfume, you cannot spread it around without getting some of it on yourself. Share optimism with others. Be as happy about their success as you are about your own. Never kick a man who is down, or aid the gossip of the town; and if you hear of one gone wrong, think your best to make him strong. Always remember to let your light shine.

4. Keep on the Move

"The road is always better than the inns."

There is nothing permanent in the world but change. Everywhere this law is evident. Everything in nature is always on the move. Movement teaches a great natural law. It tells you to keep on the move. It tells you to keep active. It is more fun to wear out than to rust out. Keep on keeping on. As an old proverb says: "He who tills the soil shall eat." Keep on the move. It is the real way of life. Watch the bees flit from blossom to blossom in search of honey. Observe the ant, consider her ways, and be wise. Every cell in your body is active. Everything around you is on the move, so why not you and I?

When you keep on the move, you advance. Grass does not grow under moving feet. Keep on the move and you form good habits. You turn pessimism and defeat into action and achievement. You turn negative thinking and discouragement into positive thoughts of confidence and power. You turn failure into success. You can look to the future with interest, hope, and desire.

5. Exercise Patience

A king was seeking a motto that would act as a panacea for all troubles. He invited all the wise men in his kingdom to offer a motto. Many brilliant ones were submitted and not two were alike. The king analyzed each motto. Each one was given careful thought and consideration. Among those suggested was one that the king selected as the most inclusive panacea for all troubles. It read "And this, too, shall pass away."

This motto is the essence of patience. It denotes calm, endurance, or self-possession. Patience is the capacity to realize that all conditions and situations are only temporary; and if you exercise forbearance and remain cool, calm, and collected, the most trying ones will right themselves. Patience teaches us to grin and bear! Trials, tribulations, troubles, obstacles, delays, **disappointments**, and failures are only stalking shadows that instantly disappear in the light of patience. "In your patience possess ye your souls."

Of all the characters in history, there is one that always shines out as a true example of patience—Abraham Lincoln. During a critical period of the Civil War, when the nation was falling apart and everything was going wrong, President Lincoln sent a very important order to his most astute Secretary of War, Mr. Stanton. Secretary Stanton read the order. tore it to pieces, told the messenger that he would not fulfill the order, and that Lincoln was a damned fool for giving it. The message was taken back to Lincoln. "If Stanton called me a damn' fool, then I must be one," said President Lincoln. "I will go over and see him." Throwing his long arms around the shoulders of Secretary Stanton, Mr. Lincoln pleaded with him for co-operation. From that day on Secretary Stanton was Mr. Lincoln's best friend and stanchest supporter. Patience had won the day.

When adverse conditions cross your path, these six lines will console you, and help you to exercise patience. Shakespeare wrote:

> Sweet are the uses of adversity;
> Which, like the toad, ugly and venomous,
> Wears yet a precious jewel in his head;
> And this our life exempt from public haunts
> Finds tongues in trees, books in the running brooks,
> Sermons in stones and good in everything.

Most of us are prone to forget all things must be accomplished by a little at the time. This entails detail. Life is made up of details. It is one thing after another, and no one escapes it. Talking is detail, one word after another. Walking is detail, one step after another. All personal acts and all acts of service entail detail. The house in which you live is a mass of detail constructed in orderly arrangement. This book is a mass of words arranged in detail to present different ideas.

Everything in nature operates in detail. The silent shining of the sun conforms to detail. Ponder on the enormous amount of work it accomplishes. Millions of miles to travel, a complete solar system, including eight planets—Mercury, Venus, Mars, Jupiter, Saturn, Uranus, Neptune, Pluto, and our own earth, to heat and light and, with all these vast duties to perform, the sun can still ripen the tomato in the back yard.

It took Leonardo da Vinci over four years to complete "Mona Lisa," the most famous portrait in the world, for which an offer of five million dollars was refused. With untiring patience, da Vinci inserted every detail and captured that fleeting something we call "expression." After four hundred years, this master-piece of art hangs on the walls of the Louvre, an inspiration to every mortal.

The one way to master detail is to exercise patience. Learn to love it. With the proper attitude, chores are a very pleasant pastime, especially when you realize that everyone else is doing them. Every task begins in detail, and ends in detail. To feel kindly toward detail relieves tension and strain, develops the power to concentrate, and the task is soon completed. Relish detail, and detail loses its sting. Don't mind detail, and detail will mind you. With all your manifold details, exercise patience. It will reward you.

It is estimated that it takes less than 7 per cent of a locomotive's power to pull a train of box cars, but that it needs 100 per cent of a locomotive's power to start the train. The task, the difficulty, and the job seem to be in starting. Start something. Take stock of your ability, analyze it, and size up your place in harmony with the chapters in this book. Practice self-reliance, learn to depend and rely on your own ability. It is always where you are, and is instantly available for your use. By all means draw upon it. Let your light shine. Demonstrate optimism. Look for the best and expect the best. It is always present. Keep on the move. Gold is found by those who look for it. It is no farther away from you than the five steps in this chapter. Keep on the move. You will find it. Exercise patience. Trials, tribulations, and adverse conditions are only temporary, and patience is a ready solvent to dissolve them. All things come to him who thinks and has patience to wait.

Opportunities are as plentiful as the air you breathe, and also as inexhaustible. They are all around you. Take the five steps in this chapter and convert these opportunities into realities. Achievement is the result of invested effort. "He that loses his life shall find it." Harness your forces, measure your time, marshal your energies, and concentrate your ability on the job at hand. Lose yourself in the affairs, services, and needs of others. Make their interest your cause; let the results take care of themselves; and before you know it, your place in life will be secure. You will turn wishbone into backbone. You will crown your efforts with achievement.

Be like the postage stamp, stick to one thing until you get there. You will discover that your place is where you are, and your success is only a by-product of what you are.

Believe in yourself.

And believe in God.

Chapter 24

LET'S TAKE A TRIP TO CHICAGO

Or, if you live in Chicago, let's take a trip to wherever you want to go.

I want to discuss with you: Prophecy and Precedent in the Realm of Faith.

A Practical Explanation of Faith

Sometimes it helps, in contemplating larger matters, to reduce them to the simplest terms. So considered, one aspect of a subject may shed light on another. Take faith in God, for example, which, particularly in these unhappy times, is a favorite target for skeptics. We know, of course, that faith in God, under a thousand creeds and in spite of every conceivable disaster and affliction, can never be dislodged from the aching heart of the world. But let us be fair to the doubter. Obviously, it is easier to believe in the life about us than in a life we cannot see. I mean it is easier in the sense of being a demonstrable occurrence from hour to hour and free from the metaphysical mists that often, and quite reasonably, discourage practical minds. Let us, therefore, leave metaphysics out of it. Let us examine faith in relation to things that we know of and can speak of in terms of our daily lives. For even the plain problem of living involves faith—not religious faith, but the simple faith of believing today in the advent of tomorrow. It may be that we can perceive some spiritual correspondence between the faith by which we live and the faith in which we die.

I may as well confess that I, too have not always been immune to skepticism, though my allegiance to it has never been complete. I have alternately denied both the Deity and the Doubt, though I invariably found it easier to believe in Something than in Nothing. I have long been of that "innumerable caravan" that cannot make up its mind. One day I believe and the next day I reject, which is, I think, a familiar phenomenon of faith. I speak here of a reasoned faith, as distinguished from blind obedience to a creed. It was ever hard for me to believe what I was told by people who know no more than I do. And that attitude, of course, is opposed to faith. It is precisely when faith consults reason that reason rebukes faith, because reason asks for evidence that faith cannot supply. Your dictionary says so. It defines faith as "belief which is not based on proof." This is hardly encouraging; so let us ask ourselves a question: What is based on proof? The answer, so far as I can see, is: NOTHING.

Let us assume that you live in New York and plan to leave today for Chicago. What makes you think that you'll ever get there? What proof have you that you'll be in Chicago tomorrow morning? None. The fact that you were there a month ago proves nothing about tomorrow. Anything can happen between sundown and sunrise, between New York and Chicago. What then impels you to believe that you will arrive? Faith! Faith bought your ticket, packed your bag, and now watches the clock to be sure of being on time. But faith proves nothing. To contend that you will be there tomorrow morning because you were there a month ago is not proof, but precedent. When you take a train this afternoon, you will be following a pattern that you have found successful on previous occasions, and which, in the light of common experience, may be indefinitely repeated. That is all. So that what your proposed journey really amounts to is this: "Belief without proof" is leaving for Chicago.

Now, it isn't even necessary to take a trip to Chicago to prove that every conscious act of our lives is based on faith. We may not stop to analyze it so, but it is irrefutable just the same. We rise from the table in the faith that we shall eat again; we labor in the faith that we shall rest again; we say goodbye in the faith that we shall meet again; we sleep in the faith that we shall wake again. Indeed, if there were no such subconscious faith in the heart of man, the race would stop in its tracks, the business of life would stagnate for want of impulse and direction, and progress in every activity would subside and cease. Analyze, for example, the day before you. What makes you think your job will be waiting for you this morning? It was there yesterday. What makes your employer think you'll be on hand this morning? You were there yesterday. What makes you think you'll meet your cronies at lunch at the same restaurant? You all met yesterday. What makes you think your family will be there to greet you when you get home? Yesterday. What makes them think you're coming home? Yesterday. What makes you think you'll take your wife to a movie, read a detective story, play canasta or the ukelele when dinner and the dishes are done? Yesterday. And so on, ad infinitum, through an everlasting reiteration of pattern that is a matrix of our footprints and an echo of our actions on the day before.

Or, let us take a more serious example, one in which faith in the world about us and faith in a world to come converge in a great Christian festival. Even those who do not believe in what Easter signifies, still believe in the advent of Good Friday and Easter Sunday. For nearly two thousand years those two sacred days have been an inseparable part of Christian experience. We may reject them spiritually, but we cannot deny them chronologically. They bring us twenty centuries of calendar proof. They are a tradition. They were, so to speak, here yesterday. And women will buy new hats and men will buy candies and flowers and children will be outfitted anew, all in the faith that what happened before will happen again; though, of course, Easter does not happen; Easter occurs. That is the distinction between prophecy and precedent: prophecy predicts; precedent recalls. Faith in another life is faith without evidence. Faith in another Easter is faith founded on experience. And yet, interpreted liberally, the basis of each faith is the same. Good Friday may be a week away, and its spiritual promise is, of course, a world away, but it is faith that sustains both theories. Easter, in the calendar sense, is a mirror of yesterday; Easter, in the prophetic sense, is a vision of tomorrow. Faith in the things of this life rests on a fulcrum of precedent; faith in another life, like the lever of Archimedes, rests on faith alone. The simplest circumstance in our daily lives is a pattern of all our yesterdays. But the supreme faith that believes in God and the corollary of another life is the light of the soul.

Recently, I, too, went to Chicago and the foregoing speculations came about in just the fashion I have indicated. A man called me up on the telephone to ask if I could see him on Wednesday morning. I said: "Make it next Monday, I'll be in Chicago Wednesday morning." And, as I cradled the receiver, that inner voice that speaks to all of us at times was suddenly audible: "How do you know?" I didn't know, of course, but the incident set me thinking. If I can believe in an earthly tomorrow, I can also believe in an eternal tomorrow, and if there is no proof of the second, neither is there any proof of the first. I resolve the matter as a tale of two cities, one terrestrial and known, one celestial and unknown, the latter requiring a little more faith than the other, only because it has not yet come within the itinerary of my travels. Just because there is a precedent for reaching Chicago is surely no reason for denying the existence of a city I have not visited before.

I believe in Chicago because I have been there.

I believe in the Hereafter because I have not been there and am in no position to deny its reality.

So, I believe in God.

Chapter 25

IT IS ALL YOURS—TAKE IT EASY

Every day I thank God for two things: First, that I was born a human being. Second, that I am a citizen of the United States. As a human being I am able to visualize and imagine my opportunities. As a citizen of the United States I am able to realize and enjoy them. This great heritage gives me cause to be truly thankful.

Everyone in the United States has cause to be grateful. No nation in all history has been more generously blessed. Most assuredly the United States is the garden spot of the world. Her geographical position, combined with her varying altitudes, provide a greater variety of soil and vegetation than any equal extent of territory in the world. There is no logical or common-sense reason for anyone to be a pessimist living in the United States, if he will only open his eyes and see.

As an individual citizen in the United States you have free access to its gigantic wealth through your own initiative and ability. As long as you do not encroach upon the rights of others, you can acquire as much of it as your capacity warrants. It is all yours.

All these unlimited resources are yours to draw upon. All these inexhaustible supplies are here to satisfy your desires.

You have the ability to convert them into economic values to meet your own comforts and enjoyment. Therefore, there should be no occasion for want, and certainly no reason for doubt, uncertainty, anxiety, worry, or dread. However, a few suggestions on how to relax and take it easy may help you.

Physical fitness, mental alertness, and personal efficiency are largely determined by your ability to relax. You are at your best physically and mentally when you are relaxed.

Relaxation is only following out a natural law. All things in nature grow with ease and grace. There is no friction. It has also been proved by observation and experience that the power of most living things lies in their ability to relax. The dog can leap three times as far from a state of relaxation. The rattlesnake can strike its full length from a state of coil or relaxation. The lion, the tiger, the panther all leap with deadly aim from a reclining position.

When you are in a state of relaxation water will hold you up. A person drowns because he fails to relax.

Relaxation tells you to loosen up, to take it easy, to relieve tension, and let go. It tells you to take the brake off, to open up, and to let the forces of nature flow into your body. These forces will restore, recuperate, revitalize, and rehabilitate you. These forces cannot enter your body when it is rigid and tense. They only come when you cease trying or straining.

Relaxation is very important to the physical body. The body is made up of billions of cells. Among these cells are the nerve cells. The nerve cells include the sensory nerves, which convey impressions from the sense organs to the brain, and the motor nerves which cause and direct movement. These nerve cells get their nourishment to perform from the blood. When they are well fed and well nourished with pure blood, they become strong, like nerves of steel. They are able to withstand storms, jolts, and hard bumps. Therefore, Chapter 9 on "How to Double Your Energy" is very important. By all means read, study, and practice the principles as outlined in that chapter. Train and discipline yourself to masticate your food thoroughly. Train and discipline yourself consciously to breathe deeply. Train and discipline yourself to take sun baths. Train and discipline yourself to drink plenty of water. Train and discipline yourself to stretch as outlined in Chapter 9 and do it systematically. When a difficult situation confronts you, take a deep breath, all your lungs can hold, and count to ten.

By following out the above suggestions you are going to have a strong body with the power to relax, to do the job efficiently. These suggestions will also help to keep you young and vibrant. They will remove the wrinkles from your face. Stretch and you feed the cells of the face with blood. Blood and wrinkles do not go together.

Everyone wants to be well, happy, teeming with energy, confident, capable, and free from care. Possibly a few suggestions on how to relax mentally may help you to realize this. Here are a few that help me.

1. Love

Love means to practice a feeling of kindness in all activity. The brain is the center of all activity that takes place in the human body, whether the act is voluntary or involuntary. The master over-all activity is the intelligence, the seat of reason.

After forty years of experience trying, testing, and experimenting with every possible motive, I have discovered that love has more power and influence over my mental activities than any other quality or attribute. When I practice a feeling of kindness, it seems to tap a great reservoir of power and strength that enables me to perform with skill and alacrity. It eliminates doubt, uncertainty, anxiety, worry, and dread and directs me without conflict or confusion. It removes all stubbornness, tenseness, and rigidity. It makes me more tolerant, more liberal, and more forgiving. It placates and soothes me. It frees me from stress and strain. It relaxes me. I can act free from all care. It pays me large dividends.

2. Know Your Business

Get a thorough, complete, and comprehensive knowledge of every phase of your business regardless of how unimportant it is. Sometimes the least important becomes the most important. Study your occupation and appraise your ability in conjunction with the chapters in this book. A thorough knowledge of what you are doing gives you confidence and this gives you the faith and power to act.

3. Get Rid of Selfishness

There are several grades of selfishness. The worst offender is carrying the world around on your shoulders. It is taking to heart everything that happens. Sympathy is all right, but false sympathy may impair your efficiency. You must learn to consider things, persons, and events impersonally, and this will help you to relax. Do not bother about other people's troubles. Most trouble will go to sleep if you do not keep it awake. Be considerate always but by no means solicitous.

4. Show Gratitude

Nothing seems to relax the mind so quickly and completely as a state of being grateful. A spirit of thankfulness for what you are and what you have seems to penetrate every part of your being. It seems to loosen the very marrow in your bones. When you stop, pause, and think for a moment. You find many things for which to be thankful. Someone has said that the Old Testament has over six hundred thousand words, and only six of these words are asking God for something. All the rest are a song of praise, thanking God for all His wonderful creation. Turn your day into a day of thanksgiving. The way to relax and be happy is to be truly grateful.

5. Train Yourself to Laugh

Laugh and the world laughs with you. Why does a man laugh? Because he has an imagination. What makes a man laugh? Because with imagination he is able to compare the ridiculous with the sublime. This quick comparison tickles his fancy and causes him to chuckle. So learn to compare and exercise your imagination. You will find many situations and conditions that will make you laugh. This will relax you.

6. Practice the Law of Averages

This law guarantees results and makes you indifferent as to results. This attitude will also help you to relax. When you have done your best, there is only one answer—results. Then too your lot or portion of life is seeking after you, therefore be at rest from seeking after it. What's the wisdom of fretting, worrying, fuming, and fussing? Billions of people have made their home on this earth for thousands of years. They tell us that all of them have been fed and sustained. They also tell us that they have not used up a thing. It is all still here. The only thing to do is practice the Law of Averages, do the job well, and trust in that inexorable law of remuneration which never fails to pay or reward you for honest effort.

The ability to relax is a great asset. It acts as a lubricant to smooth and sooth the way between all business and social relationships. It tears down and penetrates the barriers of rigid feelings. It relieves stress and strain, and frees you from apprehension and dread. When you relax, you cause others to relax. It establishes mutual understanding and confidence prevails. By all means relax and take it easy. It will give you more capacity to do, more ability to think, and more energy to act. It will take all the stubbornness, tenseness, and rigidness out of your mind and body. It will unleash all the positive and creative forces within you. It will enable you to turn your ability into cash. It will put your share in your lap.

The Declaration of Independence was a birth certificate, giving birth to a new freedom. In this certificate was hidden a dream that man could express the thoughts of his own choosing. A hope that man could perfect himself in science, in philosophy, in art, in business, in craftsmanship, or in any other field of endeavor and enjoy the fruits of his own efforts with peace of mind. A prayer that man could worship God in his own way, and share the truth of his own convictions. That dream, that hope, that prayer became your nation—America. Individual ability, individual industry, individual initiative, individual integrity, encouraged by freedom of action, stimulated by opportunity, inspired by faith, and sustained by achievement turned this dream into a reality. Today America has over one hundred and sixty-five million people who rise to call her blessed. Her cities are vast hives of thrift and industry, and her countryside is teeming with agricultural enterprise. The United States is one throbbing neighborhood of people, who live, love, and share. It is yours today—something for which to thank God.

Remember that your success lies in your dreams, in your hopes, and in your prayers. Remember also that the destiny of these United States and the future welfare and happiness of your children depend on your dignity and your nobility as a human being. Therefore, put your faith in the great creative forces within, and make every day the best day. Inspire and influence others to enjoy the abundant life with you. By planning and working together with a spirit of living and loving and sharing, America is secure, not only for you, but for your children and your children's children.

May He who clothes the lilies and marks the sparrow's fall, protect and save you and guide you safe through all!